Doing Good...

Says Who?

PRAISE FOR *DOING GOOD . . . SAYS WHO?*

As I read *Doing Good . . . Says Who?* it was as though the questions, worries, and challenges in my head were brought to life in an insightful and understandable way! As a fundraiser, donor, and board member, I found that the book has helped clarify my priorities and encouraged me to ask deeper and tougher questions of myself and others. The notions of "partnerships and surprises" will help to keep me grounded and inspired in both problem solving and strategic planning. —Bev Reed, retired VP of Resource Development, Pathfinder International

The stories ring true and are great at developing the core principles for volunteer service. This teaches people how to not only "do no harm" but also to learn from and work with communities in need. It is as important for donors as students and volunteers. —Ruth Messinger, president, American Jewish World Services

Doing Good should be required reading for all volunteers planning long or short-term global engagements. I intend to recommend it to physicians and medical students who are considering participating in global health missions and research projects. —Peter Rohloff, MD, PhD, medical director, Wuqu' Kawoq, Maya Health Alliance

Doing Good . . . Says Who? speaks with directness, wisdom, and humor to the quandary we ministers face all the time—how in trying to do good, we inadvertently hurt or harm or hold back those we want to help. The book mainly focuses on foreign outreach, but the lessons here are applicable in many, many areas. —Rev. Stephen Kendrick, minister and author

This book hits home through very concrete, specific stories from multiple viewpoints on many theoretical issues. It really helped to be let into all the aid workers heads and their dilemmas. I will definitely teach it in my class. —Emily Bauman, NYU faculty, Liberal Studies Program

Doing Good...
Says Who?

Stories from Volunteers,
Nonprofits, Donors, and
Those They Want to Help

Connie Newton & Fran Early

Two Harbors Press | Minneapolis, MN

Two Harbors Press
322 First Avenue N, 5th floor
Minneapolis, MN 55401
612.455.2293
www.TwoHarborsPress.com

ISBN-13: 978-1-63413-713-3
LCCN: 2015912287

Distributed by Itasca Books

Cover Design by Jorge Hererra with adaptations by Pat Torpe and Nancy Bingham

Typeset by B. Cook

Printed in the United States of America

CONTENTS

INTRODUCTION

Here is a story we have been told. . . .

A doctor was visiting a jungle village. After ten years of treating members of the tribe, he was frustrated. He'd spent many hours each year impressing on the chief the importance of latrines. The chief would promise to build latrines, but on the next visit none were in sight. Instead there was more waste polluting the river, their only source of water.

"Chief," the doctor said, "I'm bewildered. For years I've been telling you how latrines will make your people healthier. Please tell me why you don't build them."

The chief replied, "*Estimado doctór*, we do not understand. You want us to dig a hole, build a box, sit on it, and fill it with *mierda*. We just don't know why you want us to keep it."

Despite a decade of camaraderie, there was much the doctor and chief were missing from each other's perspective. Would the doctor have made more progress if he'd brought in a team of volunteers to construct the latrines? Maybe not. We know of another village where families were given outhouses, which are now happily being used as storage sheds.

How do any of us go about recognizing what we don't understand in another culture? How can we know whether our efforts are actually "doing good?" Does it matter? In the stories that follow, it matters.

This book is about people of good will who want to improve the lives of others in a culture not their own. It is equally about the people they seek to help, and the complex interactions that occur across their cultural divides. In the western world, those interactions are often described as "givers" helping "receivers." But this book is about a different model: partnership. We've seen better outcomes with collaboration, which challenges the effectiveness of the charity model.

The stories in this book take place in Guatemala, where we have lived and worked for a combined sixty years. Volunteers in Africa, Asia, and throughout Latin America have shared similar stories, as have volunteers from Boston, Denver, and all around the U.S., suggesting that the truths in these narratives go beyond borders.

Doing Good . . . Says Who? focuses on those who come and go—individual volunteers, donors, NGOs (non-governmental organizations), and mission groups—and the people they try to help in Guatemala. The outpouring of goodwill that fuels their efforts is inspiring. Ninety percent of North Americans believe it is important to be personally involved in supporting causes in their local community and globally.[1] Millions of everyday people are traveling to faraway places, or just down the street, to "do good." They come for an hour or a week, a summer, or even several years. Millions more make donations to organizations that "do good" and, perhaps, hope to someday volunteer their own time and efforts. As volunteers and donors cross the bridge from their side of the cultural divide, they meet locals with resources and strengths beyond their experience. This book is for all of them.

You'll join volunteers on a medical mission team, who find themselves without patients when neighbors put a hex on the clinic. And you'll accompany a U.S. businessman as he's forced to confront the unintended consequences of his generous ten thousand dollar check to a struggling Maya[2] woman.

Guatemalans have their own stories to tell. A young mother pleads, "Please don't give my children candy and coins; you are turning them into beggars." And another says, "We are not less because we have less." An Indigenous leader says, "We don't much like NGOs, because we don't want somebody telling us what to do."

---

1 Poll, *Orlando Parade*, March 7, 2010.

2 Authors note. We have chosen to use the word Maya rather than Mayan, because indigenous leaders in Guatemala prefer it.

Two lifetimes of working in cross-cultural education, human rights, and community organizing plus volunteering at home and abroad have made us passionate about learning how to connect in more than one world. While living and learning about "doing good" in Guatemala, we've met hundreds of people of good will dedicated to improving the lives of others. We've seen some unexpected results from their efforts. For instance, we met a doctor who had just finished training a group of midwives. He left totally frustrated, telling us, "Most of them slept through the workshop. Maybe it's their lack of education, or maybe they don't give a damn." Later we learned that none of the Maya women were Spanish speakers, and he had no idea that they didn't understand him.

Another example came when we met a six-foot, four-inch language student on his daily hike. He'd been noticing a group of *campesinos* (farmers) bent over their short hoes and shovels to work their land. Thinking about it from his angle made his back hurt. So he found long-handled tools to give them. When he delivered his purchases to the *campesinos* they seemed most appreciative. He went home feeling good, albeit broke. What he never knew was that the diminutive *campesinos* couldn't get leverage with the new tools. They were nevertheless pleased, because they cut off the handles and used them for much-needed firewood.

When sponsors come to visit their scholarship students, they usually bring gifts. NGOs urge them to follow guidelines designed to maintain equity. However, program directors have told us that generosity often gets the best of donors, causing them to slip a needy family a wad of cash, which, unbeknownst to the donors, often creates jealousy and a myriad of other problems. In one case, a family claimed they needed to pay up six months of rent or they would be evicted. Without consulting the nonprofit, the donor gave them what they asked for. He left without knowing that he'd been conned. He also didn't realize his gift was more than the annual salary of the staff person who was translating for him.

We've seen the likelihood of "doing good" increase when foreigners listen and learn from the local people before they act. We want this book to bring their viewpoint to light. Yet, even with our years of experience in Guatemala, we know we can't shed our Western worldview. The question is, *Can we really get into the shoes of people in another culture with our big feet?* We're still foreigners to the Spanish speakers and the Maya speakers. Realizing this hubris, we prayed for empathy and understanding while interviewing and writing.

We interviewed four hundred and thirty Guatemalans and foreigners, individually and in groups. We recorded conversations with local employees of NGOs, people in the communities where they work, short- and long-term volunteers, donors, NGO founders, and board members. The interviews cut across a broad geographic swath of Guatemala, with the majority taking place in Maya villages and most within a fifty-mile radius of Antigua, Quetzaltenango, and Lake Atitlán.

Aware that Maya in the more remote villages might be reluctant to tell us what they really think about foreigners coming to try to make things better, we worked with trusted locals who interviewed them in their own language and led group discussions with fishermen, healers, and young people. Additionally, Maya who had suffered oppression seldom told their stories, fearing more violence. We wanted to shield all the people we interviewed from repercussions and assure their safety. So we promised anonymity and went beyond the usual precaution of changing names and locations, by deciding to attribute their experiences in different settings without losing their truth. That led us to combine the interviews into the stories you'll find in this book. For example, in chapter two the narrative about the clinic comes from scores of conversations with local staff, villagers, and foreign professionals in and around five different clinics.

We took many additional steps to authenticate the meaning and spirit of what we were told. Consistently, the people who inspired these stories have confirmed that we "got it." (See the Appendix for details of our methodology.)

Five guiding principles, fundamentals for "doing good" in Guatemala or elsewhere, emerged from the interviews and provide the framework for each chapter. The stories that come from those interviews are designed to give the reader a realistic, on-the-ground, and often messy experience of each principle. The principles are at the heart of guiding good intentions into productive outcomes. While all five are woven throughout, one is a primary focus in each narrative.

1. Respect and Value People. The reader will explore what a Maya woman with a sixth-grade education can teach a donor who approaches poverty with Handi Wipes and a retired U.S. school principal with years dedicated to helping Guatemalan school children. The three of them work together to create a nutrition program that changes the lives of mothers and children in remote mountain villages, despite the challenges that come with change.

2. Build Trust Through Relationships. When a young Maya mother and her baby die in childbirth, tensions rise among older and younger generations, within families, and among local midwives. Will the new clinic be able to bridge these differences? The reader will follow a young volunteer through the ups and downs of building trust in the community, and in keeping well-meaning, short-term medical volunteers tuned to the local culture rather than their imported standards.

3. Do "With" Rather than "For." How much can *campesinos* in a coffee cooperative, an impoverished Maya mother with a micro-loan, and a Maya community working together on a reforestation project do for themselves? How do prospective donors see their work? The reader will struggle with Stanley, visiting with a group of business professionals, as he confronts the unintended consequences of his generous handout of ten thousand dollars. Where will this money go and why?

4. Ensure Feedback and Accountability. The board of a microfinance organization has done everything right . . . research, expert advice, and due diligence. Dramatic growth is underway and from where the director and the board sit, all indicators look good. So why does the local staff tell another story? What are they seeing differently? How will it impact results?

5. Evaluate Every Step of the Way. Stephanie, a New Yorker out of her element, takes the reader along with her as she learns by trial and error . . . who to listen to, when to act, and how to evaluate the impact of her efforts. Why can't she convince the *curanderas* (healers) to start a business based on their expertise with herbs that will increase their income? What do the *curanderas* see that she doesn't?

The Conclusion shows how the guiding principles provide a roadmap for "doing good" effectively. Here, we use our personal experience and examples from experts to substantiate each guiding principle, illustrating how "doing good" applies across many countries and at home as well as abroad.

The Discussion Guide is a tool to assist readers in analyzing the stories from multiple points of view. We hope the questions will provoke readers to ask their own questions and find their own answers to Doing Good.

CHAPTER ONE

RESPECT AND VALUE THE PEOPLE
We are not less because we have less.

Rapid clicks of a camera catch Amalia's attention. She looks up and sees a foreigner hastily shifting his lens away from her.

"Do they think we don't see them?" she asks her husband.

The surreptitious snapshots will show Amalia wearing a soft green *huipil* (blouse) exquisitely embroidered with birds. The intricate shadings of feathers, beaks, and eyes make them appear ready to take flight. Cristobal's traditional three-quarter-length pants also reflect Amalia's skillful stitching.

"What do you suppose they know about us from those photos?"

"Maybe it depends on what they want to see," responds Cristobal.

Morning light dances on the blue water. It casts shadows on the volcanoes, revealing shapes from Maya myths for those with eyes to see them.

The scenery is momentarily lost on the tourists as they concentrate on keeping their balance while stepping down into the rocking boat. Cristobal and Amalia sway in their seats, waiting as it slowly fills with passengers. Today, as frequently happens, more foreigners than locals are squeezed into the open-air *lancha*. Blue jeans and khakis are interspersed with *cortes* (woven skirts) and *huipils*. Cameras and suitcases compete with avocados and pineapples for every available square foot.

Cristobal watches as a couple of foreigners point to their suitcases buried beneath crates of tomatoes. They appear worried as they interrupt the boat captain. Clearly not understanding them, he smiles and waves them toward empty seats.

"I suppose those foreigners don't speak Spanish," comments Cristobal. "We both remember how painful that was."

Amalia stiffens at the memory of the blows to her head and shoulders from the teacher's stick. She didn't understand a word he said. Her papa told her that being the first in the family to attend school in Spanish would be hard. It was more than hard. But because of what had happened to her grandfather, she knew why she had to go. When he cut sugarcane on the coast, he was sure he was being cheated out of his pay. But he couldn't speak or understand the *ladino's* (non-indigenous) language and was powerless to do anything about it. Even now she can hear him say, "We need to be able to work with dignity in both worlds."

The hopes that she and Cristobal hold for their children rest on those same words. They have managed to find scholarships to put each of their three children through high school. But their youngest son wants to be a doctor. Today they are traveling across the lake to check on a scholarship possibility for him.

The motor starts. A young man heaves a rope back into the boat as it slowly pulls away from the dock. Amalia prays silently, "Thanks to God, may we all have a safe journey." Looking past the lake to the mountains that encircle it, she adds prayers for gentle rains to come and nourish the land and their lives.

§

Less than an hour later, Amalia and Cristobal have landed. They follow two local women up a lakeside path bordered by wisteria. The trail branches off to the village center with small shops, a school, and a church. At the scholarship office, Diane, the founder of the program, welcomes them in her gringa-accented Spanish. Amalia and Cristobal respond slowly in Spanish with Kaqchikel rhythms.

Diane has lived here long enough for her hair to turn from auburn to gray. In fifteen years she has learned the color-coding and patterning of the *traje* (traditional dress) unique to each village around the lake. She puts her visitors at ease by asking about the weavers in their village. They also chat about today's wind, waves, and passengers. As the proud parents come to the point, Cristobal explains that they want to find a scholarship for their son, who is at the head of his class, studies hard, and has wanted to be a doctor since he was little. As he finishes, Cristobal leans forward and says, "We would expect to repay you. We may have no money to send our children to college, but we work hard. We'd like to offer to do whatever you might need."

Amalia adds, "I cook, clean, and weave. I've taught literacy, nutrition, hygiene, and self-esteem."

Diane does a double take. She can't think of a time when a parent has offered to repay a scholarship. Neither has she met an Indigenous woman with Amalia's teaching experience. Diane pulls some papers from her desk drawer and hands them to Cristobal. "These will give you a list of our requirements, and I've included an application form. You'll see that applications are due by October next year. If I can raise enough money between now and then, we'll probably award ten scholarships.

"We don't ask families to repay the scholarships, but your offer gives me an idea. I'm going to need a translator. Amalia, maybe you'd be interested. Let me tell you about it . . . it's about that *aldea* (small village) at the top of the mountain. I was invited up there about a month ago to meet the community. When I asked them to tell me what their dreams were for their children, I expected they would ask me for scholarships. No, they wanted their children's teachers to show up for work.

"I mentioned it to my friend Ellie. We're both retired school principals and she's as curious as I am to find out why the teachers don't come to school. She supports my scholarship program, and she's coming from the U.S. to visit me next week. We want to find out what is going on up there. Would you come with us and translate? Of course, we'll be glad to pay you for your time."

After consulting briefly with Cristobal in Kaqchikel, Amalia says, "I'd like to do it."

§

A week later, Amalia, Diane, and Ellie are winding their way up to the *aldea* in a rented van. Farmers work on hillsides so steep that it is hard to imagine how they stood up long enough to construct the terraces where corn, beans, and potatoes are sprouting. Ellie points to one man who is actually roped to a tree while hoeing a small patch of steep land. As the van travels higher up the bumpy dirt road, the fields give way to pines.

Turning to Amalia, Diane says, "This is a long drive, but it will give us time to talk and get to know each other better. We'd love to hear about your family and your work. I'll stop occasionally to translate for Ellie."

"I'm not sure where to begin?" says Amalia. "My family has lived in the same village for many generations. My father, my grandfather, his grandfather, and I have all cared for the same piece of land. We were seven children. I'm the oldest, so I was the second mama in our family. I helped with everything . . . washing, making tortillas, caring for the little ones. My grandpa also taught me how to grow our food and speak with the earth. I learned weaving from my mother. When I had ten years, I began to sell our *huipils* in the market across the lake. After, I would buy some tomatoes, soap, or a little fish, to bring to the family or resell in our village."

"Did all the children in your village work that hard?" Ellie asks.

"*Si*. Everybody had a lot of work to do. My parents taught us that working hard was just part of our being thankful. They thanked for everything the day presented. They thanked for the sun, the rain, and the corn. They thanked by lighting fires, candles, and incense."

Diane translates this to Ellie who is reminded of her grandparent's farm and Thanksgiving at their table.

"Thanks to God, I was hired to teach reading and writing to women in the village just after I graduated sixth grade. I was very young. I was teaching people so much older than I was. It was upside down. They called me teacher, but listening to their stories, I learned more than I did in school.

"When I went to school, my teacher made me feel like I didn't know anything. I knew that I wanted to teach others in a different way. So I made their learning come from what they already knew. I would ask them to share a favorite story from their lives. Then I would translate it into Spanish and read it aloud. We would practice over and over, word by word, until they could do it themselves."

As an educator, Diane imagines Amalia doing that with the women in the *aldea*. "When I met with you and Cristobal last week, you mentioned something about teaching nutrition and self-esteem. Was that with the same women?"

"No, that was a few years later. I was asked to do a thirty-minute community radio program about healthy cooking, taking care of children, and self-esteem. I wanted the women who were listening to value themselves and their work, to know that learning doesn't just come from schools."

"You were what, sixteen by then?" Diane asks.

"Yes, but that job didn't last so long. It was during The Violence. At that time, the military targeted the radio station and everybody connected to it."

Like most North Americans, Ellie doesn't know much about those years. Diane tells her, "From the '60s to the '90s there were thirty-six years of violence in Guatemala. The guerillas wanted land reform. That meant taking on the elite and the military, who owned and controlled the country and the land. The military killed whole villages of innocent men, women, and children, calling them "subversives." The guerillas and the army chased one another back and forth over land that one side wanted to keep and the other side wanted to liberate. Thousands died and hundreds of thousands fled.

"When I moved here in '96, it was a little before they signed the Peace Accords. I didn't learn details until later, but I do remember that you could smell fear in the air. It's not like anything I can even describe, but Amalia knows what that means."

Understanding how painful the topic is, Diane asks Amalia if she is sure she wants to discuss The Violence. Amalia responds that so many people are afraid to talk. It's not even in the schoolbooks. That's why she and Cristobal have decided they will talk about it, because people should know.

Slowly and soberly Amalia begins. "It was absolutely the worst time in my life . . . and Cristobal's. The military thought the radio station was cooperating with the guerillas, which I don't think was true. Personally, I wasn't involved in anything political. But, the soldiers came looking for me at my house. They threatened to burn it down if my family didn't tell them where I was hiding. Nothing is more important to me than my family. I couldn't let that happen . . . so, I turned myself in." Amalia stares out the window, as Diane quietly translates for Ellie.

Ellie thinks about how much courage this must have taken. She asks, "What happened to you?"

Amalia continues looking out the window. "They took me to the coast. I was their prisoner, cooking and cleaning for a squad of paratroopers. After eighteen months, my father finally was able to sell his land and pay for my release."

"Were you married at the time?"

"Oh no, we were *novios* (sweethearts). We married later. During *La Violencia*, Cristobal was "disappeared." He simply vanished. We didn't know if he was alive or dead. Later we learned that he had been kidnapped and was tortured for some months. Then he was forced to join the military. They ordered him to murder his own people. It was kill or be killed." Brushing a tear from her cheek, Amalia sighs deeply, "It killed a part of him."

Ellie is speechless, but after a few moments she asks, "But why did they take him?"

"We don't know for sure. Cristobal is very clever and was just beginning studies to be a teacher. He had built a portable solar stove as a school project, which would use less firewood. Maybe, the military decided he made it for the guerillas to use. Of course, they were mistaken. Like me, Cristobal has never been involved in anything political. It's much too dangerous."

"Is he a teacher now?"

"No, that dream was lost. Cristobal's father died while he was "disappeared." There was no money for school. Besides, it took him a long time to recover. Until the fighting stopped and they signed the Peace Accords, he was terrified that he'd be kidnapped again. Even now, he has nightmares. His arms never fully recovered from the injuries, so he can't lift heavy things. His hearing was partially damaged, because they cut off part of his ear. But, thanks to God we are still alive and we are together."

Neither Diane nor Ellie know what to say. Words in any language seem inadequate to express their feelings. "I'm so sorry," is Diane's choked reply.

After several minutes of silence, Ellie asks, "Do you think The Violence touched the people we're on our way to visit?"

"Yes, most Maya villages were affected in one way or another, some more than others. But time has passed and the young ones only know what they've been told."

Ellie tries to take in what she is seeing and hearing. Even the landscape is so different from the flatlands of Kansas she calls home. She glimpses a patch of vibrant magenta in the small village ahead just as a pickup truck full of passengers and large bundles speeds by, cutting off her view.

Entering the *aldea*, Ellie notes that the magenta radiates from bougainvillea surrounding many homes and pathways. Some children spot the van and run alongside, giving them a cheerful escort. Other children run off to fetch their mothers. By the time they reach the soccer field, there is a crowd of perhaps fifty people. The women wear the traditional *traje* of their village in shades of red, orange, and the same magenta as the bougainvillea. Many are carrying babies in shawls on their backs. Ellie sees barefoot, dirty children. Diane and Amalia see the vibrant smiles.

The arrival of visitors is a novelty. A few teenagers bring brightly colored plastic stools. Some of the women recognize Diane from her previous visit. They urge the mayor's wife, one of the few of them who speak Spanish, to bid the visitors an official welcome. The mayor himself is out working in the fields, along with most of the other men, so Doña Marcela observes the customary courtesies.

"We remember when you came to visit us. We are glad you have returned. We welcome you and hope you will make yourselves at home." She smiles, inviting them to sit.

Amalia helps Ellie and Diane say, "Thank you" and "We're happy to be here" in somewhat mangled Kaqchikel.

At Diane and Ellie's prompting, Amalia asks the women to talk about their dreams for their children. There is a brief hum of Kaqchikel as the women consult one another and begin to speak.

A diminutive woman with a lavender apron starts somewhat hesitantly, but with growing fervor, "The mayor and the *cocodes* (town council) worked hard to get us a school. But what good is a building when the teachers only come when they want to? If we could speak Spanish, we would make the teachers do their job."

Other women chime in one at a time. "I didn't go to school," the first begins shyly. "I want my children to speak Spanish," she continues, pointing to the two thin boys beside her. "Then they will be able to work in other places, because our land is having trouble feeding us all."

"My husband speaks some Spanish. He goes to town and sells the potatoes we grow," says a young mother nursing a baby. "I went with him once. But I felt ashamed when I couldn't understand half the people. I haven't gone back. We have three girls. I want them to have the words I don't."

"I want my child to be a school teacher who will work in this village," another mother adds.

"I think one of our teachers needs a good wife from this *aldea*, who can teach him Kaqchikel!" proclaims a grandmother to the delight of the other women.

Diane and Ellie have to wait, because, instead of translating, Amalia begins a rapid exchange with the grandmother, until titters and rolling laughter overtake the gathering. "We were just teasing each other about all the tricks we know for catching a husband," Amalia explains.

As the crowd disperses, curiosity overcomes a skinny little boy with stringy hair. He sidles up to Ellie, and puts his arm next to hers. She is startled and fishes some Handi Wipes from her purse. Diane puts her arm on the boy's boney shoulder and whispers to Ellie, "It would be better to do that later."

Doña Marcela apologizes if Carlitos has bothered her. "He's always been one of the most curious of all our children. He has never met anyone who looks like you. He left school to come see you for himself."

"Is he old enough to be in school?" Ellie questions.

"He has eight years."

Her face registers surprise and concern. "He looks more like a four or five-year-old," she whispers to Diane.

As Doña Marcela leads the way on the dirt path toward the school, Ellie is deep in thought. The bright beauty of bougainvillea contrasts with peeling paint and scavenged construction materials. "These houses would fall apart in a strong wind," Ellie remarks. Diane nods, but doesn't pursue it.

Along the way Ellie and Diane stop to watch a cluster of children headed up a nearby barren hillside dragging some big sheets of cardboard. The children jump on the cardboard and slide down the hill. Shouts of glee rise above the clouds of dust following them.

Pointing to the cardboard, Ellie says, "Next time I'll bring some plastic sled discs for these kids." Diane laughs, "But, why? They're having a ball with their own sleds. I wish all kids could entertain themselves so well with so little."

They catch up with Doña Marcela and Amalia at the new school. It's recess. Two *ladino* teachers look past the women in *traje*, welcome the foreigners, and lead everyone into a classroom. They settle into short chairs at a long table. Diane notices Mickey Mouse posters decorating the concrete block walls. She's seen the same in many schools. Where do they all come from?

Diane explains to the teachers that they have been talking with Doña Marcela and other mothers about their dreams for the village's children. She asks the teachers what theirs are. They say that they want their students to come to school.

With translations flying back and forth, the teachers complain that attendance is erratic. Many students have trouble paying attention, probably because they're hungry. Diane and Doña Marcela counter that parents are worried, saying it's the teachers who aren't coming to school. The teachers explain that washed-out roads and teacher meetings often keep them from getting here.

As children stream back to their classrooms, Diane says, "Thank you for speaking with us. It helps to understand your concerns. We'll be back."

Going down the mountain, Ellie says, "I can't get my mind off Carlitos and the other skinny, filthy kids. They remind me of those gut-wrenching TV ads of starving children. Now I want to adopt every child in that village." She takes a long, deep breath. "Such poverty! There's no excuse for letting those poor people go hungry. How can we see that and sit idly by?"

Diane puts her hand on Ellie's shoulder. "You've always had a big heart. I admire how much you care and that you put your money where your mouth is. I remember when we were both school principals in Wichita and the tornado wiped out that mobile home park on the edge of town. You spearheaded the effort to help those families. So I know how much you can do when you have a mind to. Tell me what you're thinking about doing here."

"I just want to cry when I see how poor they are. I want to feed them. Can't we do something like we do at my church? We buy food in bulk, cook it, and serve it to the homeless every Wednesday night."

"Well, here there's no church kitchen and no bulk food to be found for fifty miles, or more. But we can figure something out. What I'm worried about right now is that I think we may be seeing it differently. You're seeing poverty and dozens of Carlitoses. I'm seeing people who want to do something for their kids. You're talking about handing out food. I'm talking about helping the moms themselves do something for their kids."

"But would the moms turn down food?"

"Of course not. But there are other ways to do it . . . "

Ellie interrupts, "But these people are so poor. And these kids are hungry right now. Can't we just feed them?"

"The people don't think of themselves as poor. The mothers see themselves as fighting for their children. The children don't even know what 'poor' is. It took a little boy to teach me that. My caretaker's ten-year-old, Gerardo, hangs out at my house sometimes after school. We talk, play games, and he helps me with chores. One afternoon he told me about the new volunteer at his school. He said he really liked her but he was bothered about something she said. He asked me, 'Why did she call me poor? What does it mean? Why doesn't it feel good?' I wish you could have seen Gerardo's face, when he said 'it doesn't feel good.' It sticks with me. It's so hard, but we can learn to see the person before the poverty. If we don't, it can be insulting."

"Okay, okay. I think I get it. But what can we do now?"

"Let's ask Amalia what she thinks."

Amalia says, "Yes, it can be insulting." After a moment of reflection, she adds assertively, "We're not less because we have less. For example, we had a feeding program in my village that brought together all our talents. The men built a kitchen at the school. The mothers formed cooking teams, making hot meals every day. The children brought firewood and their own cups and saucers. The NGO provided food, menus, and got everyone brushing teeth and washing hands."

Diane and Ellie begin talking over each other, seeming to forget Amalia altogether, until Diane says, "Amalia, Ellie wants to start a feeding program for the children . . . like the one you just told us about. She is confident she can raise the money. I can supervise it. But as she just said to me, it won't happen without you. You speak the language. We see how you make the women laugh and how they respond. Eventually, it would become a full-time paid job. Would you be interested?"

That program did so much for my village, Amalia thinks to herself. How could I say no to this one? "Thanks to God," she responds, "I'd like to do it. I will talk it over with Cristobal."

§

Within a few months, everyone in Ellie's church, book club, and Pilates class has heard about Carlitos and the need to start a nutrition program in the village where he lives. Their contributions along with her own and those from her family have combined to provide the funds to get the program started. Diane has shared the good news with Amalia and she has accepted the job. The two of them have traveled to the *aldea* a couple of times and tapped into eager involvement from mothers.

After several more weeks of preparation, the program's launch day arrives. Amalia knows how important it is for the women to feel comfortable with her and with each other. She'll do it the way she always does, making them laugh and joining them in their work, including washing dishes and making tortillas.

She starts with a hygiene lesson, telling the story of *Maraquita Cochinita, The Friend of Everything Dirty*. Maraquita loves to play in the mud. She would rather play in the pigpen with the pigs than to come out and play with others. She hates to wash. Other children hold their noses when she comes by. By the time Amalia gets the children to dramatize the big bugs that go after Maraquita, everyone is laughing. At the end of the story, the mothers and the children are acting out ways to get Maraquita out of the pigpen and cleaned up.

"Good!" exclaims Amalia, who is having as much fun as the mothers and the children. "Now let's invent some games so you can practice at home." Handwashing and toothbrushing charades, relays, and races follow.

With each passing week, Amalia sees more scrubbed faces and combed hair. So many women join the classes that they have to bring their own stools from home.

§

Weeks turn into months. Soon, it's been a full year since Ellie's first trip and she is returning to Guatemala. She and Diane arrive at the *aldea* with five donors, who want to see the impact of their contributions. Each guest is presented a small bouquet of flowers with a loud, "Thank you!" in English coming from the mouth of a small Mayan child. Thirty children hold hands and sing to them.

Ellie is thrilled. She keeps saying, "I'm blown away by the changes. The children are so different with washed faces and combed hair. They look healthier, too." Ellie watches as some of the mothers add mounds of carrots and potatoes to chicken bubbling in a giant clay pot. Other women are cutting up watermelon for dessert, while the children line up for handwashing. "You've done all of this," she exclaims to Diane and Amalia. "I've been getting your monthly reports but this exceeds my wildest expectations."

"Yes, the women are taking on so much more responsibility and have achieved so much."

Amalia adds, "Thanks to God, the mothers' committee is now buying the food and getting it to the *aldea*. They organized themselves into teams, review the menus with me, and do the cooking for our lunches and the school snacks. They keep the accounts straight and every week I get their receipts."

Diane tells the visitors that lunch is ready. As everyone settles on an assortment of stools and wooden benches, bowls of hearty soup arrive. Amalia directs the distribution of vitamins to pregnant mothers and toddlers. Ellie, Diane, and the donors watch as one of the mothers gives a little speech and Amalia begins the nutrition lesson in Kaqchikel.

It appears to be a dynamic between "good" foods and "bad" foods. When posters of candy, chips, and colas appear, mothers yell out "*Mahon* (No)!" Just as Amalia's colorful drawings of vegetables, fruits, and frijoles elicit a chorus of "*Utz* (Yes)!"

Then Amalia calls the children to sing a farewell song. Everyone applauds as Amalia leads the visitors down the hill to tour the school.

Ellie is pleased. Every class has a teacher and a full complement of students. "What a difference. How did you do it?"

"It was the food program. Kids didn't want to miss the lunch. Teachers realized that if the kids were coming regularly, they'd better show up, too. Of course, it probably helped that they knew I was watching."

As the van winds back down the hillside, the visitors chatter about the children and their mothers, who in many cases look like children themselves. "They are so young! How can they even know how to parent?" questions one of the donors.

"You're right," Diane responds. "But remember, many of them started taking care of younger siblings at an early age, becoming second moms like Amalia did in her family."

Ellie and the donors are firing questions at Diane and Amalia, slowed only by the need for translation. Ellie asks Diane, "How did you make this happen?"

Diane laughs and says, "Without your fundraising, there would be no program."

"Yes," Ellie interrupts, "but also if Amalia hadn't agreed to the job and you hadn't visited the *aldea*, we wouldn't be here now. It's like a three-legged stool."

"Thank you, Ellie. That means a lot. But I think the stool has four legs, because the moms are the ones making it happen every day. Amalia tells them it doesn't make any difference if they have a diploma on the wall, they are always their kids' first teacher."

Turning to the group, Diane says, "Hopefully, you've gotten a good idea of what your support means to the women and children here. I trust you can see what your dollars are doing."

"We see it and more," says Ellie. "In fact, we've been talking about raising money for more *aldeas*. We already have pledges from this group, as well as their commitment to find new donors. What do you think?"

Diane's mind races. Her thoughts are conflicted. The need is huge. Her first instinct is to help as many women and communities as she can. But her commitment to scholarships has been left on the back burner. Diane realizes that if she were to start food programs in other *aldeas*, the scholarship program would suffer even more. Yet, she hears herself saying, "How can we say no? Villages are lined up wanting to participate. Your generosity is extraordinary. Let's see what Amalia says."

Amalia is also of two minds but speaks only one. She wonders how she'll keep up with her work at home. Aloud she says, "Thanks to God, the need is so great. I want to keep helping my people."

§

Ellie has flown back to the States, and Diane and Amalia sit across from one another at Diane's large office desk, as they do each Friday. Photos of students in the scholarship program smile down at them from the wall. Amalia takes a moment to envision her son's photograph among them. He was selected for one of the ten scholarships for the coming year.

Diane asks, "What do the women in the *aldea* have to say about the visit from Ellie and the donors?"

"The mothers are so pleased . . . but they tease that I'd better teach the children some new songs, because they won't stop singing the ones they sang that day."

Diane says, "The donors loved them, too. They left with new appreciation for our work and are backing it up with money. So we are ready to grow. They want us to add three new *aldeas*."

"How do we choose new *aldeas*?" responds Amalia. "So many want us and have need. How do we decide?"

"You're absolutely right, that will be hard. But first, the thing I think about," says Diane, her brow furrowing, "is that our work will double even if we add just one *aldea*. The two of us can't possibly do it all, even if we wanted to. We both have other responsibilities. You always have a lot going on at home. This will mean more travel for you, and I simply need to get back to spending more time on the scholarship program. We're going to need some help."

Amalia has already been worrying, but when Diane says their work will double, her stomach churns.

Diane, who has years of experience taking charge, planning, and problem-solving, continues doing just that. "I figure, most of my time now is spent here in the office doing all the financial work, plus meeting with you. We're still a small operation, but the expansion will more than quadruple the amount of bookkeeping and reporting. We'll need budgets for each *aldea*, financial reports for donors, and a newsletter with pictures." She sighs, "We'll be required to do much more extensive reporting to the U.S. government for tax purposes, and Ellie wants to apply for grants, too. We're going to be swamped, but if I can find a good person to help me with the accounting finances, we can get it all done."

Most of this is like another language to Amalia, who has never heard of the IRS and has never been in a position to hire staff. She feels uneasy. When she worked on the literacy project with the elders, her boss showed her how to do the bookkeeping. She has been proud to manage the purchasing for the *aldea*.

Diane smiles warmly at Amalia, saying, "But enough about my work, let's talk about what help you'll need."

It's hard for Amalia to answer. She relies so much on the relationships she built with the women. She cannot imagine handing that over to someone else. But, as the mothers gain skills, some of her time is freed up. Perhaps she could step back more.

As though reading her mind, Diane says, "Even though you've turned a lot of responsibility for the meals over to the women, you're still pretty busy with the teaching and following up with individual families. Might an assistant help you with that?"

"I'm not sure. I guess in the new *aldeas* an assistant could review the menus and shopping lists. She could be with the cooking teams while they prepare and serve the meals. Or, maybe she could spend time with the children, teaching them songs and games."

"I'm thinking about someone you already know. It's Irma, the one you talk with when she comes to clean my office and do her homework. She is one of my smartest scholarship students, a leader in the youth group, too. She graduates from teachers' school in a couple of months and will be looking for a job."

"I like her," Amalia says. "She reminds me of my daughter, who is already a teacher. If she takes the job, I'd have someone with me who already knows the ins and outs of life in remote *aldeas*. Until she graduates, I was thinking that for now Mahón Poc would be the easiest *aldea* to add. It's close to the first one and I could probably work in both of them the same day of the week."

"They've already petitioned us to come there," agrees Diane. "I remember when they first heard that children were getting fed and mothers had their own classes in the neighboring *aldea*, they came to see for themselves. I think you could start getting the mothers organized. I'll talk to Irma and see if she's interested."

§

Two months later at the regular Friday meeting, Amalia reports to Diane on the inauguration of Mahón Poc. "I did the same first hygiene lesson . . . I love watching the children as they make all the sounds of Maraquita and the pigs in the pigpen."

"Oh, I wish I could have been there," Diane says wistfully. "I don't want to miss the next inauguration. We still need to decide where that will be."

"Before we talk about more expansion in the *aldeas*," Amalia begins playfully, "I have some other expansion to report . . . in my family." Diane puts down her agenda and leans forward to look at Amalia. She is sure her colleague is past menopause. "It's Liliana and Benjamín!" Amalia beams. "They are going to bless us with our first grandchild in a few months." Delight comes pouring out of Amalia. "I don't know who is more excited . . . Cristobal or me! Thanks to God, the *comadrona* (midwife) tells us that both the baby and Liliana are healthy."

Diane quickly comes to her feet, circles around the desk, and gives Amalia a warm, celebratory hug. "Congratulations. That's wonderful news! I remember when they were married and moved in with you."

"Now we'll be four generations in our home, just as we were when I grew up. It's working out well for all of us to be together. Liliana is a weaver, too. She works in the same cooperative I started. A baby in the house again is *maravilloso* (wonderful). It has been so long."

"Let's toast the new baby with a cup of hibiscus tea," suggests Diane, heading off for the little office kitchen. While she brews their favorite drink, Diane struggles to take in the news that Amalia will be a grandmother. Even though she may be fifty, it's hard to think of her as old enough. She seems as lively and playful as many of the teenagers in the *aldeas*.

Steaming cups in hand, Amalia and Diane drink to the health of the new grandbaby.

Diane jokes, "Just think of all the smelly diapers that are going to stack up."

"I don't mind diapers and I don't think Cristobal does either. But he teases me about 'having to sleep with a grandmother!'" Putting down her tea, stroking her hair, and miming a model's pose, Amalia adds, "I'm thinking of covering up these few streaks of gray. Or, maybe weave a new *huipil*—or just put some extra chile in his soup."

Diane laughs and wonders if the chile is an aphrodisiac or a touch of mini-napalm to bite him back with. "Well, that baby is going to change a lot of things, and I look forward to hearing all about it. For now, I guess we'd better get back to work. I've got some news, too. Yesterday I interviewed a girl named Jamie who looks like a good candidate for office manager. She worked for an NGO in the U.S. and has experience with the kind of reporting we'll need, even grant writing. She's been volunteering at an orphanage in the city for two years and has a Guatemalan boyfriend, which is why she wants to stay longer. She's willing to accept a local salary, lower than what she made in the States, and her Spanish is pretty good."

"I'm glad to hear that. Having her will help you a lot," responds Amalia.

The conversation shifts back to the choice of the next two *aldeas*. "The mothers in Mahón Poc organized themselves so well and so quickly. Three leaders put it all together, signed up the mothers and everything."

Diane says, "That's it. Strong leaders are the key for selecting the next *aldeas*. We can ask each group how they'll go about organizing the mothers in their community. Eight *aldeas* have applied for the program. Over the next month, we'll visit them and select two."

§

Jamie moves into the small office next to Diane. She has placed three photos of her boyfriend on the desk and started organizing the financial reporting to meet U.S. requirements. Privately, she looks askance at the makeshift way they've done things, resolving to make it more professional and to make life easier for Diane and Amalia.

Amalia is confused when Jamie tells her she needs to set up a separate bank account. Until now, Diane has deposited her salary, her travel allowance, and the money for pots, pans, and food together in her personal bank account. Now she must go to the bank and fill out all those papers, when it seems to her that things have been working just fine. Jamie said something about the auditors not liking it if the program's money were mixed up with her family's money. Don't they trust her? She's proud of having always been trusted.

§

Soon Irma is settling in as Amalia's assistant. She and Amalia are on their first trip together to the mountain *aldeas*. Amalia is trying to decide whether to say anything about what Irma is wearing. This *aldea* is so far away and they are very traditional and wear *traje*. They probably rarely, if ever, have seen a woman in pants.

She thinks about her own children and how she felt when her daughter started going to weekend university in Xela. After a few classes, Berta explained that it was so cold she needed to wear pants. Of course, she always wore *traje* at home, regardless of the weather. But Amalia began to notice more of the young girls had begun to dress differently. As much as she values education and the opportunities it brings, it also seems to go hand in hand with the loss of more of their traditions. The girls have less time to weave. They see other girls in short skirts and jeans on TV, and they go to the city where things are different.

Fortunately, when she introduces Irma to the women on the cooking teams and then to the big groups for classes, they don't seem bothered by her attire. They quickly take to her, probably because Irma starts joking with them right away. Amalia is glad she didn't say anything. She's becoming fond of her new assistant.

Amalia is not as fond of Diane's new assistant. Jamie keeps badgering her for receipts. In the past, Amalia herself wrote down how much she spent for transportation, food, and pots and pans. She tried to collect receipts from the cooking teams, but it was not easy to get them for what they bought in the market. How do you get receipts for fifty bananas, twenty avocados, or ten pounds of tomatoes, when none of the vendors even have paper or a pencil? She gives the mothers their own receipt pads, which they can fill out and have the seller sign, but things are complicated by the many who are unschooled and sign with an "X."

§

At the end of their visits, Amalia and Diane choose Rukux Ixim. In three more months the village's leadership team has organized more women and taken on more responsibility than in any other *aldea*. They do the shopping and cook the food. The fathers have built an open-air meeting place where they can hold classes and keep dry in the rainy season. They call it El Centro de Nutrición . . . "El Centro" for short. It has a dirt floor and posts and beams that support donated plastic roof panels. A small storage shed houses pots, pans, and a stove. A big washstand (*pila*) sits outside, not far from the unique addition to El Centro: a real flush toilet, which Ellie had insisted they install. Irma and Amalia make lots of jokes about the toilet being for the gringos who only come once a year.

One day when Amalia and Irma arrive to unlock the storage shed, the door is askew. It only takes a moment to see the lock is broken and all their chairs, pots, pans, and other supplies are gone. Even the toilet is missing from its concrete pedestal . . . its pipes carefully disconnected. Someone clearly planned to use it again. Only the stove remains. It must have been too heavy to carry off.

As the mothers with their babies trickle in to the meeting, they discover what has happened. There's a louder and louder buzz, like a disturbed beehive.

"Who would do this?"

"I bet it's the evangelicals on the other side of the river."

"Yeah, they're jealous."

"No, it must be the mayor's children. They're thieves and never get caught."

"Or the mayor's people."

Amalia quiets them. Clearly there will be no class or lunch today.

She uses her new cell phone to call Diane who responds incredulously, "What? Call the police!"

"No, no," says Amalia, "they are known to protect the wrong people in this village. I worry they're the thieves themselves."

"Well," says Diane, "I'm with a student right now, but I guess there's nothing I could do if I came anyway. Can you and Irma come to my office in the morning and we'll figure out what to do next?"

"We'll be there."

That afternoon, Irma talks to a former classmate, who is from Rukux Ixim. She tells her that the one thing she's sure of is that some of the women must know who did it.

At home that night Cristobal holds Amalia, listens to her, and cautions her to be careful with the mayor. "I've heard bad rumors about him."

"*Saber* (Who knows)," she responds. She and Cristobal have handled so many challenges in their years together. She prays for strength. There will be no program unless all the stolen goods are retrieved. Amalia resolves to take Irma with her house to house to share that decision, keep an eye out for missing items, and find out what the women know . . . or at least what they might be willing to tell them privately.

§

Jamie is bent over the books in the office. Her frustrations have been mounting. Diane is never available to help her. She's usually off visiting scholarship students in their respective schools. Ellie and the treasurer in Wichita have been calling daily, pressuring Jamie for reports that are late again. The donors are particularly interested in getting the overview for start-up expenses in Rukux Ixim, which depends entirely on receiving Amalia's receipts. She just needs the receipts, yet Amalia keeps insisting on creating a ledger before she brings them to Jamie. It's a time-consuming and superfluous task.

IRS deadlines are pressing in on them, and now that Jamie is on staff to streamline accounting practices, Ellie can't comprehend why any deadlines would be missed. Her increasing aggravation shows in her voice. *Little does she know*, thinks Jamie.

During a particularly difficult conversation with Ellie, Jamie's emotions get the best of her and she blurts out, "Look, I don't know what to tell you! Amalia is out trying to find the stolen stuff and I can't get . . . "

Ellie's voice goes up an octave, "Stolen stuff?"

Immediately Jamie realizes her mistake, but there is no way to take back her words. She tells Ellie the whole story.

"What? What happened? Everything is gone, even the toilet? That's a lot of money. We just bought all those things!" Ellie hangs up and calls Diane with an agitated stream of questions. "Why wasn't I told? What do the police say? Can't the mayor help? I don't know if I can raise that money again!"

Diane waits until Ellie takes a breath, and says, "Calm down, old friend. Let me tell you what we're doing. There was no reason for us to get you all upset when I'm confident Amalia and Irma will find everything, and soon. It's a village. Almost everybody knows everybody. I'm sure some of the women know what happened. We just have to give them a safe way to tell us. Besides, the mothers love this program; they rely on it. They know it won't continue unless all the stuff is returned. Listen, Ellie, try to relax. We'll keep you posted, I promise."

Late the next afternoon, when Diane returns from the schools she's toured that day, she pulls up a chair in Jamie's little office.

"What happened?" She asks.

Jamie's words tumble over each other. "Oh my God, I'm so sorry! The minute I told her, I was sorry. She was pressuring me for the reports, which are always late because I can't get Amalia's receipts, and I lost patience. I'm caught in the middle, and I can't get my job done."

"Whoa," says Diane. She had no idea how Jamie was feeling. "Sounds as though there's a lot I don't know. We both have had some tough days. Let's go get a couple of beers at the *tienda*. We can take them down by the dock, watch the sunset, and talk some more."

They settle back with a cold Gallo. It dawns on Diane that she has given Jamie practically no support, a situation she vows aloud to correct. "But tell me, what's the problem with Amalia?"

Jamie takes another sip and sighs, "I just can't figure it out. The first thing is she doesn't get her receipts in on time, even though I remind her frequently and well in advance. When she does bring them, her ledger sheet is a mess with numbers scratched out and re-entered. The expenses never quite balance with the income." Diane frowns as Jamie continues.

"I developed a new form that I thought would make it easy for her, but she doesn't use it. I suggested she just bring me receipts and let me do the rest, because her time is more valuable working with the women. But for some reason, she keeps bringing her damn ledger sheet . . . and always at least a week late."

"Well, easy to understand it this time, given the robbery. Besides, we shouldn't expect accounting to be her skill set. She only finished the sixth grade. She has extraordinary gifts for connecting with the women. She's the heart of the program. We don't really need her doing the numbers. Just do the reports yourself using her receipts."

"That's what I end up doing," says Jamie, "but how do I get the receipts?"

"I'll tell her that we need the receipts on time whether there's a ledger or not."

Jamie silently wishes this will solve the problem, but expects Diane will make more excuses for Amalia, protecting her because she's Maya.

"Enough about work. I love this time of day here. How are you and your boyfriend enjoying the lake?" Diane's query is gentle. She has noticed that his pictures are missing and senses there might be more to Jamie's mood than work.

"The lake is beautiful, but the boyfriend doesn't look so good anymore. I'm trying not to think about him. Things were going great. Then his sister told me—in the past two years he's proposed to two other gringas . . . he just wants a visa. I don't know what to say."

Diane has heard this story more than once. She hopes this doesn't mean that Jamie will leave.

§

As she searches house-to-house through Rukux Ixim, Amalia catches a glimpse of something shiny and white, peeking through some trees. She walks closer and finds herself at the construction site for the mayor's new office.

Sure enough, behind a barbed-wire fence amid sheets of tin roofing, lumber, and stacks of concrete blocks, hides a white porcelain toilet. Cristobal may be right, Amalia thinks.

Nervously, Amalia calls Diane and Irma. They gather together back at the office. Amalia has learned the hard way not to get involved in anything political. "You never know what they'll do to you," she explains. "The mayor could accuse one of us, raise taxes, spread lots of rumors *y saber que más* (and who knows what else)."

"You can't let him win!" blurts out Diane. She catches herself and says more calmly, "The women have to decide. They have a choice."

"I have an idea," Irma adds. "In my leadership training group, when we were teenagers, we came up with a list of demands . . . things that would make our village better, like scholarships, and trees to hold back the mudslides. The mayor wouldn't even meet with us. But there was an election coming up, so we went to the other candidates, who agreed to support our requests. Then we went to the local community radio station, got ourselves on the air, and told the story, urging people not to vote for the mayor. Immediately he responded that there must have been a mistake. He agreed to everything on our list!"

Amalia is thinking how far things have come. Now a person can be on the radio without risk of being kidnapped. Even her own kids, despite knowing her story, probably wouldn't be intimidated by speaking on the air.

Diane reminds her that if the women decide that the program is worth the risk of confronting the mayor, then whatever happens the decision will be theirs.

Two days later, all fifty mothers meet at El Centro. Since the plastic stools are gone they gather in small clusters of friends and neighbors, all talking at once. Some of the younger children are slung on their mother's back, others are darting in and out in the swaying sea of maroon and purple *cortes*.

Like a preacher shouting out an altar call, Amalia sings out a Kaqchikel greeting and gets everyone's attention. She quickly gives the assembly the details of their discovery, repeats that the program can't continue unless their equipment is returned, and asks the mothers what they want to do.

"We'll just march over there and take it back!"

"No, no, the mayor will do something to us; he's wicked."

"If all of us show up, what can he do?"

"We've got to do something! This is for our children."

Diane asks, "Is there a way you could approach the mayor without putting your families in danger?" She turns to Irma, encouraging her to share her story. The women listen.

Holding the hand of her toddler, a young mother responds. "Maybe we could all go to the mayor's office. We could tell him we think some thieves, probably from the other side of the river, put our things on his office site to make him look bad! We'll tell him . . . "

"We could go talk to the other candidates, the way Irma and her friends did," interrupts a plump mother with a wide-eyed baby peeking from her shawl.

"*Sí*, the mayor will support us for sure then."

"Why don't we tell him the program might move to the other side of the river," interjects another.

Ideas Ping-Pong back and forth across the gathering, until a plan emerges and each woman has pledged to join in and keep their plans secret so that word won't get to the mayor.

§

Early the next morning the mothers meet Irma and Amalia at El Centro, wearing their best *cortes* and *huipils*, many carrying babies on their backs. They walk together in solidarity to the small plaza outside the mayor's office. A few are holding hands.

Inside the mayor sits with his cronies, swapping stories and making plans for the upcoming election. All of them are in dark trousers, white shirts, and shiny black shoes. Cigarettes, mustaches, and potbellies complete the uniform.

Three mothers have been selected as spokespersons. Finding no one at the secretary's desk, they knock on the open office door. The mayor stands up behind his desk, takes off his glasses, and with a thin smile, asks how he can help.

"Good morning, Señor Alcalde," begins Doña Delfina, a young and feisty mother of sturdy proportions. "We're sorry to interrupt you, but we have a problem. And, we think you have one, too. You know about our nutrition center and how much it is doing for the community."

"Yes. I do," he responds with an ingratiating smile.

"We have come to tell you that all of our equipment, even our toilet, has disappeared. We are afraid your enemies might be trying to make you look bad. Yesterday we saw that someone had put everything we're missing at the construction site for your new office."

The practiced bland expression of an aging politician serves him well as he takes a step backwards and waits for them to continue. The men around him suddenly appear to be paying more attention.

"You may be the victim of a nasty trick. We think this is some kind of mistake that you'll want to correct." Planting her feet wider apart, she points toward the plaza and says, "We have more than forty women and some children outside who can carry most of the things back, but we want to make sure no one accuses us of stealing. And," she finishes, "we'll need some help with the toilet."

The two other spokeswomen add, "When we found the equipment on your property, at first some of the mothers were afraid you might be responsible. They wanted to talk to the other candidates for mayor and ask them to help get our things back. In the end, we agreed that you wouldn't want to be accused unjustly."

He pauses, and composes himself. Without looking back to his cronies, he responds, "*Estimadas señoras*, this is a truly serious matter you have called to my attention. I'm going to find the robbers. Meanwhile, my men will bring all of your equipment back to you today."

"*Gracias, señor Alcalde*," says Doña Delfina, as she and the women remain planted in the doorway. "Let's do it now. There's still time to feed the children today, if we start right away."

Half an hour later, Amalia is on the phone. "Diane, I wish you were here. I'm now in the middle of what almost looks like a parade. The mayor's assistants are carrying our toilet. Doña Delfina is walking next to the mayor, each of them carrying an armful of pots and pans. Whenever he edges to the sidelines, Doña Delfina is right with him. People are coming out of the houses to look."

§

On Friday, Amalia and Irma arrive at the office. While they are retelling the story, Jamie notices that Amalia is carrying a box. She crosses her fingers.

Amalia and Cristobal stayed up late last night figuring out how to use the new budget and expense report. Jamie has taught her that the numbers need to balance. After many tries, they finally got it right. They included her old ledger sheets, too. Jamie keeps telling her that she doesn't need to do this paperwork, but she knows it is her responsibility. Also, she wants to be sure the numbers are correct. Proudly, she hands the box to Jamie.

Jamie glances and sees that Amalia has adjusted the budget numbers to match actual expenses. Noticing that Amalia seems very pleased with herself, she takes care with her response. She'll just show appreciation and do the report herself, as Diane suggested. Amalia doesn't ever need to know.

§

Two weeks later, the staff is about to attend the inauguration of the fourth and last *aldea*. Diane greets everyone. "*Buenos dias*! And a good day it is. Can you believe how far we've come?"

Amalia adds, "I'm remembering all the mothers . . . the ones who cook the meals, the ones who got the teachers to show up for school, and the ones who marched next to the mayor and a toilet." They laugh at the image. "Thanks to God, so many children are fed and so many mothers now hold their heads higher." Looking at Irma she says, "And Thanks to God, today I get to sit and enjoy myself while you introduce the mothers to Maraquita Cochinita for the first time."

Diane looks at Jamie. "I am so glad that you will finally meet the mothers and children." Diane is hopeful that when Jamie sees how Amalia connects with the women, she'll begin to respect her more.

Today the boat is half full, with only a few tourists. The *lancha* thumps gently against the tires on the dock as Diane and the others board. She, Amalia, and Irma head for seats at the rear, but Jamie meets a friend up front and sits down to talk with her. The two tall young women with long blonde hair wear the jeans, T-shirts, and sneakers, which even the younger Maya generation seems to be adopting.

By contrast, the brilliant threads of Amalia's favorite *huipil*, the green one that's like a moving aviary, again catches the eyes of the tourists. When one of them turns his camera on her and begins snapping pictures, she thinks back to that day over three years ago, the day all of this began. Her work with Diane and with the mothers and children has been wonderful in so many ways. Yet she feels tired and pulled in different directions. She sighs deeply. With three *aldeas*, now four in roughly three years, the furrows in her brow have deepened. She dreads each time she has to turn in the receipts and ledger to Jamie.

Amalia longs for more time with the new grandbaby, the rest of the family, and her weaving. Cristobal worries about her headaches. Last night he reminded her, "You and your health are the most important thing to me. If you want to return to weaving you should. We've survived on less before, and we can again."

A gust of wind nearly sends Diane's wide-brimmed hat into the lake. She grasps it and leans back in her seat. She watches the morning light on the rolling waves. And she watches Jamie and her friend in animated conversation. Is she complaining about work? Diane is thankful for Jamie—she is a big help to her. She's adept at tracking their finances, if a bit impetuous. Diane's thoughts are interrupted when she hears Irma beside her softly practicing her Maraquita Cochanita presentation under her breath. Diane remembers that Ellie will be eager to see photos of the inauguration. She calls to Jamie to join them and asks a tourist to take their photograph together.

It will show the four of them smiling and linking arms. Each of them sees through the lenses of different cultures, generations, and experience. Yet they are together in the same boat, heading in the same direction, at least for now.

CHAPTER TWO

BUILD TRUST THROUGH RELATIONSHIPS
Go to the people. Live with them. Learn from them.

Whack! Thud! The crack in the crumbling wall opens wider and adobe pieces fly by as Lucy lands one more blow with the sledgehammer. She is amazed at her own strength.

Her commitment is to volunteer for two years. So far, Lucy has only been here for a few weeks. Her boss, Ralph, described her job as "coordinating and translating for groups of doctors and nurses (*jornadas*) who will treat patients at Clinica del Pueblo (the People's Clinic)," a church-sponsored clinic in the mountains of rural Guatemala. Other volunteer groups will arrive to help renovate the clinic. What she didn't understand, however, is that the "building," which Ralph described as "needing repairs," is a shambles with collapsing walls, no roof, and no electricity. There is no staff and no renovations are scheduled for at least two more months.

That means twenty percent of her first year as clinic coordinator will be over before anything happens. She takes another swipe at the wall, which clearly doesn't offer the building any structural support. She sighs and pauses long enough to gather up her long brown hair and hitch it into a ponytail. Where will her own support come from? Once more she asks herself, *Should I just go home?* "No!" she shouts back to the adobe wall. Then more calmly, she steadies herself and continues systematically swinging the hammer.

That night as Lucy literally falls into bed, she considers the irony. Gringos doggedly doing things their own way and knowing what's best is exactly the opposite of what she intends. For her graduate degree in Global Health, she studied many projects that failed because North Americans went in having all the answers. They barreled ahead without regard for the perspective or the reality of the local people. She came here to learn how to break down barriers between cultures. That won't happen with a sledgehammer.

Her first priority is to get to know people in this Maya village. Currently, she commutes an hour daily to the clinic site, arriving sometime after the farmers have left for the fields and leaving just as they return. She likes her furnished apartment back in town and understands why Ralph and other international volunteers live there. There are even enough foreigners to support a gringo grocery store. There's always someone to take a hike or party with who speaks her own language. But Lucy's instincts tell her to live in the village where she will be working. She wants to immerse herself in the local culture, to listen to the people, and to find out what kind of clinic could serve the village's health needs. They probably want one with walls and a roof, she thinks.

Her friends in town and even Ralph with his years of experience running clinics here try to dissuade her, cataloging their worst fears as her own. "It will be lonely. A single woman isn't safe. You could be robbed . . . or worse." She smothers her sense of insult. She knows they mean well. The last thing she wants is to be cocky or naïve. In fact, Lucy does feel vulnerable.

Toting only the backpack and computer she has brought from St. Louis, she temporarily moves in with a local grandmother, who rents rooms for occasional visitors. Hopefully, she'll find something more permanent soon.

Should she try to live with a family? It would feel more secure. She has fond memories of the family she stayed with in Mexico during her high-school summers. They would laugh together as she struggled to learn Spanish and she couldn't get enough of their hot chocolate with cinnamon. She volunteered there, too, at the nearby church-sponsored clinic. The stories she heard from the patients changed her life and made her adamant that health care is a human right . . . particularly for those who can least afford it.

Lucy learns that about three thousand, five hundred people live in her Guatemalan village and only four of them are foreigners. One local family offers to rent her a room, but the father and mother plan to move their four children in with them in order to accommodate Lucy and bring in some cash. Even if she did rent from them, she fears she could accidentally create jealousy if she stays with one family and not another. She decides to find her own place.

Within the week, while Lucy is buying bread at the bakery down the block, she meets one of the foreign volunteers. She learns the lanky Norwegian is departing after two years of working with a weaver's cooperative. She's been renting a house, which she suggests could be just what Lucy is looking for. It is. It's simple, with one room, a bed that doubles as sofa, one straight chair, and a two-burner cooktop on a wooden table. It has a flush toilet (yeah!) and a cold water shower (ouch!), both out back. There's a little bit of land out there too, where Lucy imagines herself reading in the morning sun, raising a few chickens, and perhaps growing some vegetables.

Maybe this backyard is where she'll use her USB Internet modem and start emailing the States for more volunteers and church donations. But first she'll contact her parents who are worried about her and looking for an excuse to visit. They'll want to see where she's put the little wood-sculpted guardian angel they sent with her when she went to Mexico. Her dad, who's an engineer and handy around the house, will love the sledgehammer. Her mom could help to create a small garden. Lucy chuckles to herself and decides she will wait to get the chickens until they've gone.

§

Past the market, behind the church, and down the hill, three women with small children move along the path to the river. The colors of their Maya dress interplay like segments of a kaleidoscope. They are on their way to wash clothes. Lucy doesn't know them yet, nor does she have any idea how much local gossip gets churned during this laundry ritual.

Sarita is tall for a K'iche woman, beautiful with high cheekbones and large brown eyes that shine. She's known to be very smart and helps her husband, Carlos, keep the books at his barbershop. After sixth grade, she got a job with the government distributing food to the *ancianos* (elders), where she has been working for over a decade. With Carlos, she has three children: five, seven, and eight years old.

Clara and Sarita have been best friends since childhood. After their graduation from sixth grade, Clara got a scholarship to *básico* (middle school). Few in this village can afford to go beyond primary school. It made her an ideal candidate for the job she took with an international NGO that brought groups of eye doctors and dentists to the town. Clara's Spanish is quite good, so she translated between K'iche and Spanish. Her face and her body are rounder than Sarita's, and her long black hair free-flowing. One gold tooth adds sparkle when she smiles. Her husband works with his father growing corn and beans on their patch of land. Their two children are five and seven.

Petrona became friends with Sarita and Clara at church. Today her six-month-old is nestled in a rainbow shawl on her back. She tugs gently at her mother's long braids, which are entwined with bright blue and green ribbons. Petrona's face reflects strength and wisdom beyond her years. Like her mother before her, Petrona is a midwife. During their many conversations at the river, she has confided in Sarita and Clara about how she tried hard to avoid her calling. Petrona, like *comadronas* for hundreds of years before her, was born with the "cap." Whenever a baby girl emerges with a thin membrane of skin on top of her head, the town celebrates that God has brought them a new *comadrona*. She's expected to learn the prayers and the skills, which will care for the body and soul of mother and baby, while honoring the ancestors.

Sarita and Clara were both delivered by Petrona's mother. While she was growing up, Petrona was constantly reminded of the responsibilities, rituals, and celebrations that come with being a midwife. Her mother had begun her own training with an elder midwife when she was eight years old. Maybe it was the fact that her mother could be called away at any time of the day or night that led Petrona to choose another path, that of teaching school. When she became a teacher, paralyzing headaches and an occasional seizure interrupted her work. Doctors could find no cause. It was the *curandera* (healer) who told her that her body couldn't stand the pressure that came from denying the calling of her birthright.

A dream finally convinced Petrona. In her dreams, like other *comadronas*, she was shown how to deliver a baby. She realized she couldn't fight her destiny any longer. She left teaching and has worked as a midwife for several years now. Her husband is pleased, because Petrona is now healthy and happy. He is a welder. Their baby on her back has a three-year-old sister and a four-year-old brother.

Today, the big topic in the village is that a woman and her baby have both died during childbirth. Sarita knows the family. She stops washing and sits on a rock.

"My friend Maria, her sister-in-law, told me what happened. After twelve hours in labor, the family was really worried. Her four other babies arrived only after a few hours. Something wasn't right and everybody knew it. Maria said they needed to take her to the hospital right away. But Ana's mother, mother-in-law, and all the grandmothers begged her husband not to do that. They thought it would be risking her life."

Petrona pauses, a dripping shirt in her hands, and asks, "What did the *comadrona* say?"

"Estela agreed with the grandmothers. She had attended the births of most of the family members in the room. They trusted her. As Ana lay there, Estela kept her hand on Ana's belly and prayed the traditional prayers. Finally, the baby came out, but he was dead. Ana was weeping and bleeding. Her husband got scared and agreed to go to the hospital. He and seven of them made a mound of blankets in the back of a pickup truck. They placed Ana on the makeshift bed as carefully as they could." The trip to the hospital is an hour long, on bumpy, windy roads.

"Ana died shortly after they arrived at the hospital," Sarita continues, as her tears mix with the wet wash.

"It's not right," Petrona says, scrubbing harder, using a rough rock as a washboard. "If they'd just gotten her to the hospital at the first signs of trouble, maybe she didn't have to die. In my classes at the government clinic, we are learning to see those signs of trouble and when to get other help. I hate to say it, but I hear some women no longer want Estela as their midwife. All I know is that some *comadronas* feel she's not open to new ideas."

Clara looks pensive, while continuing to rinse clothes. "I just wish we had emergency help right here in the village," she says with a sigh. "The nurse at the government clinic doesn't live here. That trip to the hospital is so long, hard, and costs a lot. Nobody wants to go there. You remember what happened to my mother. She went to that hospital with a break in her arm. She only speaks K'iche, but they kept yelling at her in Spanish."

Nodding, Petrona adds, "When the birthing mothers have to go to the hospital, we aren't allowed in the delivery room with them. The staff treat us as though we know nothing. We're used to working with our mothers in their homes, with their families all around them. We bring the traditional blessings. At the hospital, the mothers feel as though they're all alone in a foreign country."

"I can understand why the family was split," says Sarita, who has resumed washing. "Personally, I would want to go to the hospital. But there would be many reasons why my mother or aunts wouldn't want me to. After all, when they were born, there was no road to the hospital. Back then, can you imagine a woman in labor riding a donkey over these mountains for all that distance . . . even though the Mother Mary did it. But our grandmothers simply accepted death as God's will. There was nothing they could do."

§

Lucy wanders through the market in search of a pot and fry pan, but finds herself distracted by a pile of delectable green beans. She learns that Doña Alicia grew them herself and is the mother of the two small children playing nearby. The papaya also looks luscious, so she buys it too. Since she has no refrigerator, she goes to the market every day. She imagines these local vendors may one day come to the clinic. On the way home she stops for some fresh tortillas and a couple of neighbors greet her by name.

The whacks and thuds of her morning "workout sessions" on the adobe walls have prompted visits from her "clinic" neighbors. Clara, who lives next door, comes over to retrieve her five- and seven-year-olds almost daily. The kids love to watch Lucy work. She lets them help by moving chunks of adobe, which they play with by the hour.

What a surprise this scene is for Ralph when he comes to meet with Lucy for the first time since she moved. He certainly didn't expect a one-woman demolition team. Things usually move slowly in this culture. His plan was to rent space for the first *jornada*. He didn't anticipate having a clinic for at least a year. He wonders if he has hired a pushy gringa, who is going to piss off the people. On the other hand, he remembers that he was just as anxious to get started when he arrived in Guatemala a couple of decades ago. He's seen a lot of his volunteers come and go since then. Some he's had to keep on a short leash. Seeing villagers stopping by to chat with Lucy, and the children giving her hugs, Ralph decides to give her more running room.

She wants to speed up getting the clinic ready for the first *jornada*. He says that's not possible in two months. They compromise by delaying the arrival of the *jornada* until Ralph can schedule in the volunteer construction crew. Thanks to generous donations from U.S. churches, Ralph says he'll pay for construction supplies and Lucy can look for local clinic staff.

Ralph adds, "The most important ingredient is to hire someone who is respected and trusted in the community, so when the villagers come to the clinic, they aren't just meeting strangers. There's someone there who knows them." Lucy nods, remembering how patients at the Mexican community clinic opened up to local staff.

The next day, Clara brings some warm, freshly made tortillas. As they perch on the ledge of what used to be a window, Clara tells Lucy about her previous work helping with dental and eye clinics. Clara also shares some of the gossip. Lucy is moved by the story of the mother and baby who died in childbirth.

Reaching for a tortilla, Clara asks Lucy, "Are there plans for this clinic to have emergency help for such situations?" Slowly shaking her head, Lucy responds, "If so, it'll be a long time. First things first. For now we need a roof."

"Well, that's about all the government clinic has," exclaims Clara. "Five years ago when it opened, we were glad for a few more health services. But we don't go there much anymore, if we can help it."

"But why?"

"The staff doesn't speak our language. They don't treat us with respect. Their clothes are not our clothes. They're *ladinas* (non-indigenous) from the capital, in short skirts with high heels. Two of them dye their hair and wear makeup. They don't live here. That's not bad news, except when we have an emergency at night. And, they never have any medicine. I hear that they sell it."

Clara's frequent visits keep Lucy up on village life. One day Clara arrives with her childhood friend, Sarita. So, Lucy takes a break and offers her guests her two new red plastic chairs. She pulls up a stool for herself. This time it is Lucy who has tortillas to share. She has just purchased them from the woman down the street. They are piping hot, smell delicious, and taste even better with a little sprinkle of salt.

"Lucy, you asked me to tell you how things work here. We think you need to know what happened today, because it goes on a lot."

Sarita explains she has worked for years distributing food to the *ancianos*. She looks down at the dirt floor and then at Lucy. "I've had a bad scare," she begins, taking a deep breath. "I saw some policemen at the warehouse, stealing the food. I don't think they saw me, because I hid in the broom closet when I realized what was happening. I was shaking so hard I was afraid I'd knock something over. From a crack in the door I watched them loading boxes onto a truck. I'd heard rumors that they were stealing the food and selling it, but I didn't want to believe it. Who would steal from old people! They're the ones I care about. I love working with them. If the police find out I know, they'll probably call me the thief."

"How awful for you. I'm so sorry," Lucy commiserates. "I wish there were some way I could help, but I can't imagine what it is. It's a reminder to me to be wary of getting mixed up with the authorities." Ralph had warned her about this sort of thing.

As the weeks pass, Lucy begins to recognize that Clara could help her as an assistant at the clinic. People from all parts of the community seem to like and respect her, and in fact seek her out. Hiring Clara could be the clinic's cornerstone.

Clara and her husband discuss Lucy's job offer. She would translate when *jornadas* come, as she did for the eye doctors and dentists, but it's not clear what else her work will be. At least she could be close to home and learn something beyond eyes and teeth. The boys' school supplies keep getting more expensive. A little extra would help. They agree Clara will accept.

Each day Clara walks her boys to their school nearby and arrives at "the clinic" by 9 a.m. Over several weeks, Lucy and Clara sit together on their red chairs and plan.

"We don't want to be like the government clinic. How do we get the people to trust us?"

"Well, I can tell you how it happened with my cousin who lives on the other side of the mountain. A woman from her village came to visit. Because she spoke the same language and wore *traje* (traditional clothing), she welcomed her like a neighbor. Her visitor called herself a *promotora*. She was coming from the local clinic to find out about healthcare needs in the families all around. They talked about the children, the good foods to eat during her pregnancy, and the best herbs to use for her husband's sore throat. She and her neighbors used to be afraid to go to the clinic. Now that's changing."

"The *promotoras* your cousin talks about sound a lot like the ones I read about in Haiti . . . where they're called "accompaniers." They do a lot to prevent illness and to check in on sick patients, who have been to the clinic. I can imagine how *promotoras* could help us. Would you ask your cousin if she would introduce us to her *promotora* and her clinic . . . and I'll ask Ralph what he knows."

§

Balancing plastic tubs full of dirty clothes on their heads, the three women arrive at the river, where they find two other friends, Josefina and Patricia, already rinsing their wash. Clara tells them about the idea of *promotoras*. Sarita is excited.

"I quit my job with the *ancianos* a few days ago. I couldn't work there anymore after what I'd seen. Do you think there's a chance I could work as a *promotora*?"

"You'd be perfect, but I'm not sure if there is any pay."

"If my husband decides money is a problem, I could do some more weaving and sell it. It could be another way to help the *ancianos* and others. I'm ready to try something new. Since my youngest will be in school soon, I'll have more time," adds Sarita.

Clara gives her friend a nudge. "What if you have more babies?"

To Clara's surprise, Sarita responds, "I hope not. You remember how difficult my last pregnancy was. The doctor said another one would be very risky. Emilio and I talked about it and decided not to have more. But we're not sure what to do. We've heard all the rumors about pills, condoms, and injections . . . but, what to believe? Do you think the clinic could help us?"

"I know there's a group of gringo doctors and nurses coming. Maybe one of them can help. I'll ask. Lucy was very concerned about the death of Ana and the baby."

Josefina has been listening quietly, until she can no longer hold back. "The gringos always tell us we should have fewer babies. But they don't know us. We love our kids and want more. I understand, Sarita, why you don't want to risk more. But Timoteo and I need them to help in the fields, watch the little ones, and care for us when we're old. Besides, terrible things happen if you do what the foreigners say. They say we should take pills. But my neighbor says if you take them, the baby gets born with pills in his hand. Another neighbor says the pills stick together and make cancer. The *ladina* nurse at the government clinic told me I should stop having 'relations' with my husband. She doesn't understand. There's no way I'm giving that up."

Patricia blurts out, "My husband would beat me. He says women take pills so they can get in bed with other men. He's always jealous. I don't want to sleep with other men . . . I don't want to be beaten."

Petrona has been listening carefully. She knows that many of the pregnant mothers she cares for feel as strongly as Josefina and Patricia. They want more children, and no foreigner is going to talk them out of it.

Clara is thinking how her husband's family's land has been divided up so many times, it barely supports them and their two children. The world is changing and her kids will need to find other work. They will need to learn Spanish. It will be hard enough to educate them. What would she do if she had more?

§

Several months later, when Clara enters the clinic after dropping her boys at school, she is startled. She has never heard Lucy raise her voice before. But she overhears Lucy all alone, screaming out loud, "I'm not their fucking travel agent!" She doesn't need to know English to understand that Lucy is upset. Then she remembers that the first *jornada* is coming next week, and the volunteer construction crew still has a ways to go before the roof is on. She decides to take Lucy a cup of tea.

Lucy is, indeed, fuming about the upcoming *jornada*. She wants to spend more time working with her staff before the medical team arrives. But here she is tending to another round of tedious and largely irrelevant questions emailed by the volunteers. Somebody is concerned about what kind of pajamas to bring. Another one has heard that the toilet paper is really rough. Should she bring some? Lucy has already sent them a packet of detailed instructions for the trip. The answers are all in there. Or if not, they could have figured it out themselves.

What is she getting into? If the volunteers sound like spoiled brats on email, what will they be like in person? She recognizes that she has less patience with the professionals coming from the States, because they have so much. Lucy reminds herself that these people are nervous about the unknowns of a new place and culture. Besides, they are coming to help.

Having gratefully sipped the tea Clara brought her, Lucy calms down. Without these *jornada* volunteers and others like them, there would be no clinic. They raise the money, bring the medicines, and treat the patients. Ralph says many return or make donations because they are so moved by the experience. She vows to listen to them. She still hopes they behave better on arrival.

§

A week later, with the clinic about to open its doors, Lucy takes a deep breath and realizes that they are as ready as they'll ever be. It's far from perfect. But, the roof is on. That's thanks to the volunteer crew Ralph found. Lucy would have preferred to hire local builders, because they need the work, but the volunteer package was complete and timely. They had been given a thorough orientation and enough skills training to make them genuinely effective. They brought their own supplies and equipment and knew what to do with them. The power tools were constantly humming. They even made a contribution to pay the electric bill, something many groups never think to consider. Bringing their own translators and arranging for their own food and housing meant that they could go right to work with the local masons. They were respectful and good humored. It gave Lucy an enormous appreciation for the gifts that can come from short-term volunteers when the NGO prepares and supervises them adequately.

It was Clara's husband who came up with an ingenious solution for "private" consulting rooms by rigging up partitions of wooden frames holding blankets or opaque plastic sheeting. The clinic was ready to welcome its first medical volunteers in a real building.

Lucy contracted with Clara's friend, Maria, to cook meals for the incoming nurses, doctors, and their support volunteers. Clara and Maria planned the menus and Lucy went over all the sanitation procedures for fruits and vegetables. Lodging was arranged for the travelers at the small local hotel.

Ralph provided the funds for Lucy to hire both Sarita and Chenta. Eventually, Sarita will select, train, and supervise the *promotoras*. For now she'll mostly translate. Like Sarita and Clara, Chenta speaks both Spanish and K'iche. She has just returned from nursing school . . . a special commitment, since most who go away to study don't come back home to work. To augment staffing, Ralph will come with Daniela, the nurse at his clinic.

Lucy turns and asks out loud, "Are we ready?"

"*Si, Dios quiere.* (God willing)," Clara responds. Chenta offers a simple prayer. *This is the day*, Lucy thinks to herself. *Ready or not, here we go.*

The whole village is abuzz. The *jornada* is great for local business. The hotel is fully booked for the first time anyone can remember. Toothbrushes and candy bars are piled high at the corner store, the owner having heard that these are two items gringos always want.

The van pulls up at the clinic. A bunch of exhausted, anxious, and excited folks from Atlanta pile out. Neighbors peek out their windows.

"*Hola!*" A visitor hands out candy. Another gives children coins. Lucy winces.

Ushering them into the clinic with hurried welcomes, she invites the visitors to sit on stools arranged in a circle.

"This may not look like it, but this is Clinica del Pueblo," Lucy says, gazing around proudly. "If you could have seen it only a few months ago, you would know how far we have come. Today we are sitting in our conference room. Tomorrow it will be the waiting room for the patients we are all eager to see. Later, I'll show you what we have rigged up for consulting rooms, but for now I'll ask you to introduce yourselves and tell us your specialty."

When the visitors finish their introductions, each member of the staff follows and thanks them in three different languages.

Lucy picks up on the interplay of languages. She turns to Bill, who has just introduced himself as a bilingual doctor in a Latino clinic, and asks him to tell the group about the role of translating when doctoring.

"Before I got more fluent, the biggest challenge for me was to look at the patient. It's hard, because the natural instinct is to look at the translator. They're the one talking to you, but not the one you're there to care for."

Lucy nods. "Yes, and a couple of other things . . . like slowing down. Translations take time. Also, time is different here. At home we say 'time is money,' but here time is something you're in. It's now. It's slower. Besides, going at their pace helps us get in their rhythm. That's the relationship we want. I'd rather have word around town that each patient feels good about the experience. That's more important than the number of people we see."

Ralph inserts, "Another thing is, don't forget, we haven't got all the facilities you're used to. No X-rays. No lab. There'll be times when you'll reach for an instrument you're used to having. When it isn't there, please resist the temptation to yell at the nurse. Another thing that will test your patience is that not everyone will know the names of their body parts. For example, they will tell you they have a kidney problem, when the symptoms don't add up. Actually, it usually means they have back problems from carrying heavy loads. If you can put yourselves in the shoes of an old-fashioned country doctor asking lots of questions and figuring out the answers yourself, you'll do well here."

Lucy picks up. "Speaking of old fashioned, Ralph, why don't you talk about dressing with respect for the local customs and the other protocols."

"Here's a dress code you won't forget," he says. "Remember the 3Bs . . . no Boobs, no Bellies, no Buns . . . for males or females." Some of the visitors grin. One or two frown as Ralph continues, "Drink bottled water. Brush your teeth with it, too."

Lucy inserts. "No giveaways. No coins. No candy. Nothing. What you do here will affect the climate of our work and the expectations of the town for every team of volunteers who come after you."

Ralph interrupts, "Listen to her. It's serious. It happened at my clinic. A volunteer doctor was taken in by a charming young man on the staff. He told the doctor about how much he wanted to go to school and make something of himself. The doctor gave him scholarship money without any of our knowledge. It turns out he gave it to the least productive member of our staff, who quit and never went to school. Imagine how the other staff felt when they had to do his work, while he chatted up the doctor and pocketed the money. It isn't the doctor's generosity they still talk about. So if you get inspired to help anybody here, that's wonderful, but talk to us first." A couple volunteers squirm in their seats.

When Lucy sees the dentist scuffing his foot in the dirt, she addresses the body language. "Some of you are looking at our elegant floor. I imagine you're wishing for shiny, clean tiles. You'll probably have lots of ideas on how we can improve things. I know a lot needs doing, but please keep a running list and give it to me or to Ralph at the end of the week. That's because while you're here, our primary job is to translate for you. Other things will have to wait."

As the volunteers ask more questions, the staff passes out a copy of the week's schedule.

§

The next morning the medical team, comprised of three MDs, the dentist, three nurses, a young physical therapist, and several support volunteers, arrives in their work clothes ready and raring to go. There's an assortment of blue and green scrubs, cowboy boots and sneakers, dresses, and jeans.

Clara's father-in-law is the first patient. The doctors practically fight over him, but it's his teeth that hurt, so the dentist wins. Gradually, a few more relatives and friends of staff come through the door. Given all the anticipation, this seems like a rather paltry showing. Lucy tries to ignore the worry welling up in her. Clara confides that some people in the village are saying that neighbors have put a hex on the clinic. They are afraid to come. There's more here than Lucy understands.

Those particular neighbors have been a problem all along. It seems as though every time Lucy has resolved one issue with them another one sprouts up. Most recently, they tried to tell Lucy that the clinic had to pay them rent, because part of the building is on their land. Ralph was forced to hire a lawyer who put that to rest. Now they're saying they need a wall between the clinic and their house to protect them from all the sick people. Lucy thought she solved that problem by showing them that the patient entrance is on the opposite side of the clinic. Apparently, they're willing to do most anything to get their wall.

On the surface local staff are remaining loyal to the clinic, but they also admit to being nervous about the hex. Sarita tells Lucy, "An ex-girlfriend of Emilo's was very jealous when we got married. She did everything to break us apart. When our little boy was born, she put the *mal de ojo* (evil eye) on him. He had a fever, didn't sleep for days, and cried all the time. We took him to one doctor after another. Finally, my mother-in-law cured him with the traditional combination of herbs, eggs, and prayers."

Chenta adds, "Something like that happened to my father. A plague of misfortunes came upon him. A car ran into him . . . he was robbed . . . depression took hold of him. My mother said he'd been hexed (*embrujado*). I remember going with her and all my brothers and sisters to the home of the *Ajq'ijab'* (spiritual guide) where we all prayed for his healing and protection. He recovered."

"Don't worry," Ralph says, when Lucy tells him of the responses to the hex. "They'll get over it. Things will settle, people will just move on."

"What about the community?" Lucy argues. "Clearly, they believe there's a hex, because they're not coming to the clinic. This cloud could hang over us for a long time. Besides, I feel we should honor the staff's concerns. We need them with us. They have always lived here. They know better than we do."

"So what are you thinking?" Ralph asks.

"Well, I don't know any of the Maya priests here . . . yet. For now, I think I should go talk directly to the hexers. If need be, I think we should offer to build them a wall after they take the hex off."

Ralph shakes his head, "Building a wall would be giving in."

"Building a wall would be far less costly than a clinic with no business. Do we have enough money in our building fund for the supplies and a stone mason? Maybe some of these volunteers will agree to do the hard labor."

"Alright, go for it," Ralph capitulates; then he adds, "You know these MDs will think that this is absurd."

And, indeed, they do . . . except for Bill, the bilingual doctor. He's had more than one patient who blamed the evil eye for their ailments.

"Oh, come on, Bill. That's ridiculous. They were conning you to get meds. Can't we just explain to them there's no such thing as a hex?" Jasper, the dentist, asks incredulously, again scuffing one of his cowboy boots in the dirt.

"With all due respect," counters Lucy, "why would these Indigenous people believe you? You just arrived. They don't know you. They do know a hex. The spirits are real to them. They believe spirits can get loose and do harm. Isn't that what you're saying, Bill?"

"Oh, for Christ's sake!" retorts Dr. Clyde. "How many months did you say you've been here? How many clinics have you run? We came here to treat sick people, damn it! So where are they? If they're sick and want to get better, they'll come."

Lucy takes a breath. "I agree with you. There are a lot of sick people who want to get better. If you get ready for them, I'll work on getting them here."

Turning from Clyde to the rest of the team, Lucy is holding on by a thread. She manages to keep it together long enough to ask, "So, tell me, who's game to help build a wall?" There are a few grimaces but most hands go up. Hastily she adds, "Thanks! Meet me back here in an hour."

Lucy holds back her tears until she can escape outside and hide behind her favorite jacaranda tree. As the tears stream hotly down her cheeks, she remembers how Clyde was on her case yesterday, too. He questioned her Excel spreadsheet and insisted she'd charged him too much for the trip. He practically accused her of stealing.

They have no confidence in me, Lucy tells herself. No one takes me seriously, because they think I'm too young, too female, too inexperienced. Maybe Ralph should take over, they'd listen to him. *Enough*, she thinks. It's about getting the patients in here. She wipes her face with her sleeve, straightens up, blows her nose, and goes off to deal with the neighbors.

An hour later, Lucy has struck a deal. The physical therapist is showing the volunteers how to carry cement blocks in a way that will build muscles and not hurt them. Peter, sometimes known back in Atlanta as Dr. Santa Claus, laughs that he has never worked so hard to get patients.

By afternoon, there's a wall. Chenta suggests a blessing ceremony. In no time at all, neighbors and volunteers come to join in the ritual. As word spreads around the village, more patients appear.

Eventually, even their neighbors come out from behind their new wall to line up for anti-diarrhea medicine.

"I just hope they don't return to drinking the contaminated water," Chenta says.

"The nurse did talk to them about that," adds Clara, "but boiling or buying bottled water is expensive. They need access to clean water."

"I wish we could solve that," says Lucy. "Maybe we can put it on a wish list and find an NGO that specializes in water to take it on."

§

It's day two and Betty Sue, a librarian and Sunday school teacher from Atlanta, is pouting, her reading glasses slipping down on her nose. She came to help. She likes to be busy, but finds herself spending a lot of time just sitting and waiting for instructions. Her assignment is to manage "the pharmacy." That means organizing and handing out the medications they brought from the States. She also records these transactions. But while patients are with one of the team, she has nothing to do. She's bored, but more importantly, she feels underutilized. She thinks that these people don't seem too organized. They don't know how to treat volunteers.

Betty Sue is not the only antsy North American. *If only they spoke Spanish*, Lucy thinks. She has already had Betty Sue rearrange the medications by type and list the quantity of each. That was good for a half-day's work. Having her create a new record system added almost a day. Lucy thinks of the stories about large NGOs who sometimes resort to things like having volunteers painting the same classroom walls over and over again, four or five times a year.

There are grumps because there are not enough patients, and then there are grumps because there are too many. She reminds herself that doctors, in particular, are used to being continuously active . . . and not used to being questioned.

While she translates for Clyde, she hears him prescribe medicines for thirty days of diabetes treatment. Diabetes is a growing complication for local families who have traditionally eaten a protein-healthy diet of tortillas and beans. In recent years there has been a shift to white bread and Coca-Cola, Frito look-alikes, and Fruit Loops, especially among the children.

After the patient leaves she asks Clyde, "What do we do after your month of meds runs out?"

Clyde responds dismissively, "I think that's the clinic's problem. I've been on other *jornadas* where giving a month of medicine is the norm."

"But then what do they do?" Lucy insists. "I'm not a doctor, but I'm pretty sure that the patient's diabetes isn't going to go away after a month. Our clinic has no more medicine and no budget to continue the treatment. So tell me what happens after thirty days."

Clyde looks momentarily puzzled but honestly responds, "I don't know."

Lucy asks, "Well, wouldn't it be dangerous to give only a month of medication without any follow up?"

"What about nutrition classes for diabetics?" suggests Clyde, his tone becoming more sympathetic.

"Maybe, in the long run," responds Lucy. "But what do we do now?" Her question hangs in the air unanswered.

§

In the evening, over dinner with Lucy and Ralph, the group dissects their experience.

"If the need is so great, why weren't the lines a mile long?" Betty Sue questions. "Don't you advertise this thing? Did you send out fliers, announcements in churches and schools?"

Lucy, who has done each of these things and more, swallows hard, smiles, and thanks her for the ideas. She asks everyone for the highlights of their day.

"I thought I'd be treating more tropical diseases like I did at a week-long clinic in Africa," puzzles Dr. Clyde. "I haven't seen one case of malaria here and no one to give the bed nets I brought."

"You could find what you were expecting in the coastal lowlands," responds Ralph. "But here in the highlands it is less common, or less common than it was when there was more seasonal migration down to cut sugar cane. Whole families would go for two or three months. They lived in huge open-air sheds. The men and boys cut cane. The women and girls cooked and did laundry. They came back here with a little cash, and all too frequently with pneumonia and malaria. Their modern counterparts temporarily working on the coast are more likely to bring back STDs and AIDS, but that topic is not out in the open."

"Is anyone doing education on prevention or family planning? Did you say some of the younger mothers are interested?" asks Dr. Peter.

"Clara tells me that a few of her friends are interested, but not the older women," Lucy responds.

"I might have guessed that about the older women. I treated several of them for prolapsed uteruses. Each of them had more than seven children. I'm glad the younger generation may have more choices about their bodies."

"My concern," says the physical therapist, "is for the patients to do the exercises I've given them. Their back problems from working in the field and carrying heavy loads won't get any better if they don't do their exercises at home. What I've been able to help them with today won't make much difference unless the exercises continue, and I can't follow up with them."

Lucy wonders if *promotoras* could take this on, too.

§

A mother brings her eight-year-old boy, Eduardo, to the clinic with shortness of breath. In his "consulting room," Peter welcomes them. He sees Eduardo eyeing the stethoscope around his neck. He takes it off and hands it to him, saying, "Would you believe this gadget has ears and can listen inside you? Would you like to try it?" Showing Eduardo how to put the instrument to his ears, he lets him listen to his heart and watches Eduardo's big brown eyes widen. "Now I'd like to listen, but first I want you to jump around for a few moments."

After the exercise, it is clear that he is short of breath. Peter hears heart palpitations when he puts the stethoscope to Eduardo's chest. He recognizes the signs of a congenital heart condition, which if left untreated could kill the boy. Asking Eduardo and his mother to wait for a few moments, Peter goes off to consult with Lucy.

Peter tells her that Eduardo needs surgery. He suspects an atrial septal defect, which needs to be confirmed with an ultrasound.

"If I'm right," Peter says, "there's a procedure to plug the little hole in the heart, which may do the job without open-heart surgery. In either case, if acted on, this child should have a long life. If not, he'll likely die an early death."

"Oh no. I can't bear the thought. But, how would he get that surgery?" Lucy asks.

"What do you mean?"

"Well, we're simply not equipped to handle it. We don't have the resources or the facilities. It probably means going to a hospital in the capital. Then, there's getting the family to agree to go to the city, a place they've never been, and a hospital where nobody speaks their language and where their neighbors have had awful experiences. There's every reason for them to say 'no.' Local tradition says the extended family decides, not just the parents or the doctor. Even if they said 'yes,' some of the family would need to go with him. They can't afford a private hospital, and at the public hospital families have to bring the food as well as pay for medicines and transfusions. Their choices aren't the same as the ones we have."

"But how could the family let him die? Look, let's talk to Ralph about this. It's not right!" Peter argues.

"Well, the family has reason to be confident that he will live," responds Ralph, when they bring him into the conversation. "As they say, God willing. Western medicine is simply not a part of their reality. The reality in this village is that most who go to the hospital die. Because it's only the high-risk cases that get sent, many of them do die there. They'll probably want to protect Eduardo, to save him from all that. Clara told Lucy they're one of the few families she knows who haven't lost a child. They may feel that it is simply their time, while consoling themselves that they have other children. It's hard for us to understand their point of view, but they have a lot of experience with things they can't change."

"Well, maybe they can't change things," exclaims Peter, "but I'd like to try. If you can get the family to agree, I'll pay to get him to Guatemala City. I'll pay his family's expenses and for someone they trust from here to go with them to advocate in Spanish. I'll pay for the surgery. I can't stand by and let this little boy die."

"You're very generous," responds Lucy. "With your help I hope we can convince them. I really do. But, please understand, this is not just about money. Let's ask Chenta to explain this to the mother and see what happens."

§

During the final few days of the *jornada*, Clyde seems to forget where he is, ordering tests and X-rays not available and not affordable for this clinic. In contrast, Peter is diagnosing the old-fashioned way, using simple tools and good questions. He relates to his patients well. He picks up a local gesture and pats them on the shoulder. He tells jokes and conveys his genuine concern. Bill is also in his element, speaking Spanish with those who do and picking up some of the K'iche words from Clara as she translates. Since he doesn't need the additional layer of translation from English, he's able to attend more patients.

The dentist is pulling badly decaying teeth. He vows to raise money for the equipment to do fillings. He tells Lucy that if they get the right tools to the clinic soon enough, some of these patients' teeth can be saved.

Betty Sue continues to be in a snit. She's still ruling the roost in the pharmacy and Lucy has gotten used to her critical nature.

Lucy recognizes how hard it is for these older professionals to take her seriously. Doctors are accustomed to giving the orders and not being questioned . . . especially by someone like her. Yet most of them pledge to return next year. Lucy wonders if they will, half hoping that she does not have to endure another week with some members of this group. When she finally gets them to the airport, she sighs in relief.

§

Ralph and Daniela join Lucy and her staff to debrief. "Let's talk about Eduardo, Chenta. What does his family say about going to the hospital for an operation?" Lucy asks.

"*Pues*, they are afraid . . . for Eduardo and for themselves. They had a hard time understanding about the hole in Eduardo's heart. When I tried to explain surgery, they became more frightened. No one in the family here had ever been to a hospital or traveled farther than the next town. But, then I explained that Doctór Pedro would pay for me to go with one or two of them and help out at the hospital. They got into a big discussion. Finally, Eduardo's mom told me she has a cousin who lives in the capital and they would ask about staying with her. They must still be trying to contact her, because I haven't heard anything more yet."

"Well," Ralph says, "if Eduardo does have surgery, he and the family will need your help both before and after. You'll be a godsend at the hospital, but when he returns home, you'll need to check in on him frequently. If all that happens, the odds will be in his favor for a healthy recovery."

"Fortunately, Chenta," Lucy says, "we can spare you now as we're just getting started. But, as the clinic grows, we probably couldn't. The timing and the doctor's generosity are sort of a double miracle. I pray the family will agree."

Sarita turns to Ralph. "I'm seeing how important follow up can be, but can we do something more before *jornadas* come?"

"Before?"

"Yes, before. It's because of the elderly patient who waited in line a long time. He reminded me of when my eighty-year-old *abuelo* walked barefoot in the rain all day to get to an eye clinic. Nearly blind, he was desperate. He waited in line for hours. Finally, they told him he needed cataract surgery, but they couldn't do it and sent him home. He was exhausted and didn't understand. I think someone should have checked him before he went that far and waited that long.

Lucy listens. There are no easy answers, but she's getting a better picture of patient needs and what the clinic can offer. "After our health *promotoras* get some basic training and experience, maybe we can learn how to prescreen as well as follow up. I think I told you about my experience with Dr. Clyde and the prescription for a diabetic. I was troubled that we'd have no way to continue medication. But his idea of a weekly meeting for diabetics has potential."

"Maybe I can help you with that one," Ralph suggests. "A good friend is coming to visit me tonight. He's a doctor and has some experience in treating diabetes in Guatemala. I'll ask him his approach."

§

Back in town, tired from the week with the *jornada*, Ralph feels he's earned the bottle of Pinot Noir that he brought from the States. He uncorks it to share with his old college roommate, Brad, visiting from Boston. They both enjoy the serendipity that each has ended up in Guatemala. Ralph came originally as a missionary, Brad as a doctor.

Brad shakes his head as Ralph describes Lucy, "I can't believe you would turn the responsibility of a new clinic over to some 'do-gooder' just out of grad school. Remember when I worked at my friend's church clinic on the coast? Every week a new group of State-siders showed up in their matching T-shirts-for-Jesus, speaking English only. They photographed everyone in sight, upsetting some patients who associate the camera with evil spirits.

"The worst was that about half of them brushed their teeth with tap water and got parasites. They moaned and groaned, asked for medication, and kept our few bathrooms filled so that our patients had little chance to use them. Then they screwed up the Guatemalan plumbing by forgetting to put toilet paper in the wastebasket." The friends laugh, remembering they did the same thing at first.

Settling back in his chair, Brad says, "Patients here deserve to be treated in their own language. That's why I learned to speak K'iche and require anyone treating our patients to be fluent in their language. Untrained volunteers don't get in. The only volunteers we see are the specialists we bring in from the States to treat a specific illness. They are not allowed to see a patient without me there."

"It's a great idea," Ralph reflects, somewhat jealously. "Most of the Guatemalan docs aren't Maya speakers and they don't often come to the countryside. It's a godsend that some foreigners like you do. The only problem is there aren't enough of you to go around. Besides we couldn't afford you anyway. Lucy has hired all locals. Once trained, our promoters will visit families and can deliver basic, preventive care in K'iche."

Ralph fills Brad's glass and continues, "Lucy is fluent in Spanish and spent four summers working at a clinic in Mexico. She's a rare bird. Anyway, enough about volunteers. I want to ask you about diabetics. What do you do when you don't have access to long-term meds?"

"We think we're on to something. Given how hard it is to change bad habits by yourself, we started a weekly club to help our patients manage the disease. You've probably noticed that when they first get the diagnosis, they're overwhelmed, get depressed, and think they're done for. When we get them together to cook and exercise, they realize they're not alone. We make a big deal about finding the healthy foods they like and can help them get their systems back in balance. It's too soon to declare success, but we're encouraged they're coming to the meetings."

§

Sarita and Petrona are alone together at the river. As they finish their washing, they sit on the bank, reflecting on the changes they've seen in the two years since the clinic opened.

Petrona turns to Sarita. "One of my new mothers told me about your *promotora's* visit. She's used to my coming to her home to take care of her and the baby, but she was surprised to have somebody come from the clinic. She says you even checked her blood pressure."

"I remember," responds Sarita. "Her little boy's finger was infected. I used the first-aid kit they gave me when I finished my year's training. She was one of the first I visited. I was nervous for a while, but then I wondered how I'd ever get out of there. She didn't want to stop talking. Her back hurt and she wanted to know what to do for her husband's rash. We are asking Lucy for more training to know when symptoms are serious enough to send them to the clinic."

"I'm wondering if they could provide classes for us *comadronas* too. Maybe I'm a little jealous of your first-aid kit."

"But I hope you won't lose the 'old ways.' I loved lying on the woven mats in the *temezcal* (traditional sweat bath), with all the other mothers-to-be. We all talked while your mother massaged my belly and my back with the sacred stone."

"I know. But I have been dreaming of Ana and her baby. I never want that to happen to one of my families."

"Let's ask Lucy. How would you get the *comadronas* to come? They're used to working on their own. Like you, their calling is a gift from God."

Petrona nods. "It's a sacred trust, and some believe it's not to be shared even with each other. Some believe they don't have anything to learn outside of their dreams. But my mother and I talked this over. We think that if we visit each *comadrona* and talk with them personally, some will come because they trust us and want to learn. All we need is a place to meet."

§

Lucy stands in the clinic at the very spot where she started knocking down walls two years ago. She is just back from Christmas holidays in St. Louis. She pulls up one of the red plastic chairs, and remembers all the tortillas she and Clara have shared sitting here together. The building has been transformed at the hands of waves of volunteer groups. They've built consulting rooms, a small dental office, a large area for training, and a mini herbal pharmacy.

She's homesick. Her friends kept asking when she was coming back to the States and reminded her that her initial commitment has been fulfilled. Most of them are married and well into both family and career, also things she wants.

And yet, how can she leave? This morning Sarita and two other *promotoras* came knocking at her door, as if they knew she was feeling lonely. They grabbed her by the hand and begged her to go with them to the senior center. Usually, they just visit the *ancianos* to do blood-pressure checks. But today she watched as they basically ran a vision clinic. They had invented an eye chart. Instead of letters they put symbols, in increasing size, of things the elders see every day . . . a humming bird, corn, a carrot, a grinding stone, cabbage, a fish, a basket. Whether the *anciano* had gone to school or not, they could read it. When one of them couldn't see a symbol from the right distance, a *promotora* helped them select from an assortment of donated glasses, a gift from a recent *jornada*. Lucy wished she'd taken her camera.

Other *promotoras* are giving nutrition classes and getting a vegetable garden started. Several go into homes on a regular schedule to measure the height and weight of babies, despite resistance from the more territorial *comadronas*. Petrona and her mother now have twenty midwives meeting each week and asking for more training. Lucy has asked Dr. Bill to return and offer family-planning courses.

Yet it's a challenge to get *promotoras* to show up on time, or even show up every day, and work on a schedule. Record keeping is also new to them.

She gets back health forms on maybe every third patient. Most recently the rumor spread through town that a *promotora* had given the measles to all her clients. Now many won't open their doors. Lucy feels like she forever has to start over.

As the staff and the *promotoras* take on more and more responsibility, what is needed in her position is for someone to raise money and keep the volunteer groups in line. Neither is the part of the job Lucy is best at or especially enjoys. Besides, she's made it this long without butting heads with the mayor, the police chief, or the local priest, and the clinic isn't missing any drugs.

At this moment, Clara's son bursts through the door of the clinic, jumps on Lucy's lap, and gives her a big hug. Now she's back to feeling that she'll never be able to leave.

That evening at home eating rice and beans, she longs for some of her mom's meatloaf. She gets a beer from the little refrigerator that her parents got for her and stretches out on the lumpy sofa. She thinks about her St. Louis friends. It was so good to see them. She remembers the warmth of Joy and Jack's baby in her arms.

She knows she's growing further and further apart from those college friends. They are consumed with diapers and daycare, carpools and promotions. They barely had time to ask her about her life. When they did, they didn't quite know what to say. They admired how she's helping poor people. They praise her courage and generosity. What does that really mean? They even sent a little bit of money to the clinic. She's invited them to visit Guatemala, but no one has come.

She can't exactly go back to where she was. She's changed too much. At the same time, she can't fully belong in this culture either. Sending up a silent prayer, she asks to find a way to live and work in both worlds.

CHAPTER THREE

DO "WITH" RATHER THAN "FOR"
Never do for someone what they can do for themselves.

In the dirt yard of a small Guatemalan house, Joe stops translating in mid-sentence and his jaw drops. Stanley is pushing a ten thousand dollar check into his hand, asking him to present it to Angelica, the Mayan mother, whom they have just met. Ten grand is probably half the annual GDP of this entire village, he thinks. Joe doubts that many people in these mountains know what a check is. He looks at Stanley in disbelief.

§

When the visitors arrived, Angelica invited them into her home to show them her doll-making business. Stanley was doing his best to sandwich his ample frame between the dirt floor and the corrugated metal roof. As the rest of the group squeezed into her two-room house, he bumped his head against an unlit bulb dangling from the ceiling. The only light filtered from outside through the slats of her bamboo walls. It was almost impossible to see the dolls.

After her husband died, Angelica took out a two hundred dollar loan to start a small business making and selling cloth dolls. She coaxes uniquely shaped figures from old discarded textiles, which she stitches together and stuffs with straw and cornhusks. When she embroiders their features with bright thread, they become unique and appealing personalities, and the dolls quickly leave the marketplace in the arms of new customers.

Stanley was relieved when Angelica suggested they take the dolls outside for a better look. Angelica apologizes. "My electricity has been cut off. I was one of the few able to get it when it came to our village a year ago. The wonderful thing for me was I could work into the evenings and make more dolls. My business grew, but it is down again now. There are only as many dolls as we can make by daylight, not enough to have the electricity turned back on."

Angelica's five kids came running into the dusty yard from behind the house. Excited but shy, they drew close to the foreigners to get a better look. The oldest, a pretty twelve-year old, carried her youngest brother on her hip. She was eager to show the group a bright, cheery-looking doll, which she herself had made. Her little sister hugs another doll, pointing to its embroidered purple eyes. Putting her arm around the oldest, Angelica says, "The kids are helping me build the business."

Once outside, Stanley was breathing more freely, but was troubled by what he was seeing. These children are so beautiful and full of life. All of them living in this place you can barely call a house. Stanley's shoulders slumped and he stared at the ground, picturing his own grandchildren who have no idea how blessed they are. He was thinking how he could help this family.

Tuning back to the group, he heard Angelica describing how her loan works. "Our payments are due every two weeks, and up until now I've never missed one. But I'm worried about the next. My eight-year-old, thanks to God, is healthy again, but he had a nasty infection that wouldn't go away. His medicine took all of my savings. Now the baby is sick, and I'll need to sell more dolls, so I can pay for medicine and repay my loan."

"What will happen if you can't pay?" questioned Ed, whose banking career makes him especially interested in every angle of micro-lending.

"*Pues* (well), the agreement is that the group has to pay when someone can't," Joe translates. "They might have to do it for me this time. I've done it for them before."

Stanley could hardly contain himself. The women Angelica relies on probably have little more than she does. He thinks the least he can do for her is to give her money to pay the bills and build them a decent house. His wife, Anabelle, gave him a questioning look as he pulled out his checkbook and started writing.

§

Choosing his words carefully, Joe suggests that Stanley wait until tomorrow to deliver his check. Joe is familiar with foreigners bringing gifts, because he works with church groups who pass out a lot of them. For several years he has translated for one-week missioners who come to build houses. Here he's pinch-hitting for a sick friend, translating for bankers and realtors rather than church groups. He's more comfortable with the language of hammers and nails than of investments.

Stanley and four other Clevelanders are visiting Guatemala for a week to select which of three community projects their business club will fund. Their professional networking group takes pride in supporting projects in downtown Cleveland. But some months ago they set their sights on an international project, which led to this trip. Their first stop was to visit Angelica, a borrower in a successful micro-lending program.

Back down the mountain and settled into their hotel, the group, who've known each other for years, gathers for dinner. None of them have been to Guatemala before, but each of them views the trip as an opportunity for the club and themselves. A year after chemo treatments, Evelyn is taking more time off from her real estate business. Carl has a new assistant at his pharmacy and wants to meet the Guatemalans his son, Jack, volunteered with. Ed, the banker, is eager to explore how nonprofit loans work in a developing country. Stanley and Anabelle are both recently retired, he from his dental practice and she from teaching fourth graders. They're finally free to travel, and here they can do it with old friends.

Opening a Gallo, Guatemala's favorite beer, Stanley challenges Joe, "What could possibly be wrong about giving that family ten thousand dollars?"

Joe starts slowly in his Tennessee drawl. "That's what I would have said when I first got here. I wanted to help everybody I met. The only reason I didn't was that I had very little money. Actually, I did give some coins to kids."

"But you stopped?" asks Evelyn.

"Yes, ma'am. In no uncertain terms, one of their mothers told me I was turning her little boy into a beggar. That got my attention. It wasn't long before I started hearing other stories about good intentions screwing things up. The one that really got to me involved a hundred dollar bill . . . not a ten thousand dollar check . . . but it was enough to get a young girl kicked out of her home."

"How could that happen?" inquires Anabelle.

"Well, ma'am, a group of funders kinda like yours was visiting a mentoring project. They were shown around by a sixteen-year-old girl, who was tutoring a younger child. The older girl so enjoyed her role as mentor and tutor that she had decided she'd become a teacher.

"When one of the group commented that her family must be proud of her, they were astonished to learn that instead of being proud, her mother was angry. Her mother sold vegetables in the market and needed her daughter at home to care for her seven younger brothers and sisters. The father had "gone north" three years before. He had hoped to send money back to feed them and to send her to school. There had been no word from him since.

"One of the visitors was so concerned that unbeknownst to anybody else, a hundred dollar bill was slipped into the girl's book bag. When the mother found it, she screamed at her daughter, calling her a prostitute. She beat her, cut off her hair, and threw her out of the house."

"Surely the program director could get the mother to understand," Anabelle insists.

"No, ma'am. Nothing anyone could say would change the mother. She was convinced there was only one way her daughter could have gotten that kind of money."

"So what did the girl do?"

"Well, that's how I came to know the story. I found a safe place for her to live where she could earn her way by cooking, cleaning, and babysitting."

Stanley says, "Wait a minute. I don't want to hide anything. Wouldn't handing Angelica a check be transparent?"

Anabelle, looking pensive, says, "But honey, wouldn't the whole village see her lifestyle change?"

"Yeah," says Carl, "sort of like what happens in the U.S. when someone wins the lottery."

Joe says aloud what he'd only thought before. "I'm pretty sure her extended family would all want to move in and everybody in town would expect some help. Others might try to get a share by stealing. There's a possibility that it could put her in danger."

"Good God!" Stanley mutters, as the others weigh in.

"I'm trying to picture what she'd do with the check," says Ed. "I didn't see any banks in her village."

"Most of the ones this size don't have them," says Joe. "It's likely she's never seen a check and would have no idea what to do with it, even if there were a bank."

"Couldn't the loan officer, the one who works with the borrowers' group, help her with that?"

"Good heavens! What if that woman has family problems, too? I wonder how much she makes. Probably, not much," Evelyn adds.

Pausing for a sip of tea, Anabelle says, "Don't you think she'd be happy for Angelica? But you're right. We have no idea what her needs are. There's so much we don't know," she sighs.

"Truth is," Carl says, "the village probably won't believe how she got the money. They might accuse her . . . like what happened to the sixteen-year-old."

"Like I said, couldn't I solve that by making a public presentation of the check," Stanley insists.

"If you did, Stanley, wouldn't the neighbor's be jealous?" asks Carl. "Joe, does that happen?"

"Definitely. Let me tell you about an experience that taught me something about jealousy. Not long into my job with the mission groups, the owners of a house our church built were forced to move to another village. It may sound strange to you, but jealous neighbors said the money for the house had come from the Anti-Christ and accused the family of sinning by accepting it. The owners became terrified that they'd be punished both by God and their neighbors. They were afraid to move in."

"Can't your church do something to prevent that kind of thing?" Carl asks.

"Well, you'd think so, but the pastor, my boss, won't listen to me. I asked him how he selects families. His response was that he listens to the Lord." Joe puts down his Coke. "It appears to me he simply responds to the family that gets to him first."

"Have you seen this create problems?"

"More than once. Often while we're working on a house, neighbors will show up asking how to get one. Just last week, a father took me by the hand and led me down a few streets to his house. It was made of cardboard and many 'found' things, an old Gallo sign, corn stalks tied together, and some pieces of old canvas. It was flimsier than the house we were rebuilding. He and his wife had twice as many children in as small a space. His wife was soon to deliver their sixth child and he had been out of work for several weeks. They were as sweet as they could be. They even brought their only chair out and insisted I sit on it!"

"What did you do?"

"I had to tell them to see the pastor, because he makes all the decisions. Then I stayed awake nights worrying. I decided if the pastor wouldn't discuss these things with me, I'd probably end up looking for another job. Some other organizations building houses have a formal selection process. They make sure the community understands and follows it, by hiring a local person whom the people trust."

"Stanley, we have no idea whether in this village there are families with even greater needs than Angelica," says Anabelle, placing her hand softly over his. "We don't even know about the other women in the borrowers' group."

"I want to ask our driver, Fredy," replies Stanley. "He is probably in touch with local needs. But it's hard to believe anybody could have it worse."

"That's a good idea. We'll have time with Fredy in the van tomorrow," confirms Joe. "He and I have worked together ever since I started translating for our construction volunteers. Because he spent time working in L.A., it will be easy to talk with him. His English is good."

Not long after dawn, they all climb into the van, a bit the worse for wear after a night made restless by lumpy beds, barking dogs, and crowing roosters. Anabelle reports that Stanley tossed and turned all night. He had nightmares about Angelica and her family, then about himself spinning wildly on a Ferris wheel.

Stanley hefts himself into the co-pilot seat. It turns out Fredy has cousins in Angelica's village. He's heard about her, because she was one of the first to get electricity, something his cousins hope to have someday. His cousin's little girl has one of Angelica's dolls, which she keeps with her all the time.

"So, see Stanley," his wife says, "others never had electricity at all. They don't think of Angelica as a hardship case, they look up to her."

"Seems she's going through a tough patch right now," says Ed. "I'm struck by the fact that she was focused on how to manage it with help from her daughters and the other borrowers. With her repay record, my bank would rate her as a valuable client."

"She didn't even sound as though she was complaining, just explaining how it is and how she's dealing with it," Joe remarks. "We wouldn't have known the whole situation if we hadn't learned why the electricity was shut off."

Stanley perks up, "Then why can't I help her, if only just with the electric and medical bills?"

"Is there a chance she might not want our help?" asks Ed. "I remember loaning a woman in my AA group two thousand dollars to start a business selling snacks from a cart. I knew her very well. Like Angelica she was widowed with a bunch of kids; she was laid off from her job, and I wanted to help her. She was absolutely determined not to accept handouts. She had so much pride and didn't want pity or charity. She wanted a loan, not a gift."

"Why does giving somebody a little bit of help have to be so damned complicated?" fumes Stanley. "Fredy, how would you feel if somebody gave you ten thousand dollars?"

"Is that an offer?" Fredy grins. "Actually, I'd buy a new van and expand my business."

"I'm struck by how the women in Angelica's group support each other. Is that typical?" Evelyn asks, looking at Joe.

"Well, it's part of the loan contract, but it's rooted in family tradition here, too. In this culture, families, loan groups, and whole villages often make decisions together. Our stonemason sold some chickens to help his sister when she needed major surgery. Another brother sold a goat, and sisters in the U.S. sent money. Charity began at home, but then they all had a say about whether she should have the surgery."

"Stanley, I'm beginning to think that we see Angelica in isolation," says Evelyn. "We don't see the network around her. She and the other borrowers may have it covered."

"How about I give one thousand dollars to each woman in her loan group? Then I would be helping more people, and jealousy would not be such an issue."

"How about giving your check to the micro-lending organization, where it can help hundreds of Angelicas," suggests Ed. "The advantage of working through the NGO is they have a lot more experience with the ups and downs of their clients and know more than we do. At least they've been here a lot longer than we have, and I'm going to trust they've figured out what ways work best for Angelica and women like her."

Stanley, exhausted, closes his eyes and allows the jostling of the van to lull him into a nap. Evelyn and Joe are talking quietly as others follow Stanley's lead and doze.

Joe asks Evelyn how the club picked Guatemala for their project.

"It began with Carl's son, Jack. He'd been volunteering in Guatemala for two years. He came to do a presentation for our club. His photos of the country and the people were so beautiful . . . alongside so much poverty. I was horrified when he told us our C.I.A. got rid of their first democratically elected president."

"I know the feeling," Joe acknowledges ruefully. "It was even worse when I learned that we trained the Guatemalan military who shot whole villages of Mayans."

"Is that possible?" Evelyn questions.

"It was an ugly reality that lasted thirty-six years until they signed the Peace Accords. Did Carl's son tell you about that and the ten thousand NGOs that have sprung up since then?"

"Yes. That's when we decided to look for a business project to fund."

"Well, Guatemala is a lot closer to the U.S. than other places you might have invested in," observes Joe.

"Exactly. The geography helps. So, what was it like for you when you first came?"

Joe laughs at the memory of arriving with equal parts of excitement and bewilderment. "I was told to take a 'chicken bus.' I didn't know they meant the old yellow school buses from the States with seats made for kindergarteners. I had to fold my body into an accordion, my knees practically touching my chin. I was sharing one seat with two round Maya women holding children in their laps."

"I'd like to have seen that. Why do they call them chicken buses?"

"Chickens ride in baskets up on top along with piglets, cabbages, and Lord knows what all. If there's no room on the roof, chickens ride inside too. Baby chicks were chirping in the luggage rack above my head. A woman up front was preaching salvation and an old man in the rear was selling 'snake oil' guaranteed to heal everything. That pretty much tells you about a chicken bus, except for the crazy colors they're painted. All my worldly possessions were in a duffel on the top of that bus, and I was off on the ride of my life."

§

As the travelers step out of the van and stretch their legs, they are met by a red-headed gringo, wearing jeans, a striped polo shirt, and rubber work boots. They had not heard about his red hair. They only knew they'd be meeting a fellow who was an M.I.T. dropout who couldn't stop inventing things, whether for the high-tech corporation in the States or the large Guatemalan NGO where he worked before he came to this cooperative.

Conrad greets each of them enthusiastically, shaking each hand with a firm grip. He welcomes them to CC (Cooperativo de Café), which he helped found with the local *campesinos* (farmers). When he asks the group if they've ever been to a cooperative before, they shake their heads no. Conrad says he'll show them around and introduce them to some of the farmers, who are the ones who do the work and run the co-op.

Following Conrad in his squeaky boots, the visitors are glad to get fresh air and are eager to learn about a different business model. Joe gets a break, since Conrad takes over the translating.

They follow Conrad a few blocks to Micaela and Raimundo's home at the edge of the village. Once through the bamboo gate, they see Micaela standing next to an enormous white rose bush covered with blossoms that perfume the air.

"What beautiful roses!" Anabelle delights.

"Thank you," responds Micaela with a modest smile, "Welcome to our home. When Raimundo and I married, his parents gave us this piece of land. The first thing I did was plant the rose bush. I've watched it grow, just as our family and our house have.

"We have been here twenty-three years now. I'll show you around until Raimundo comes back from the fields."

They walk a short way along a path bordered by some aloe vera and enter what Micaela fondly calls "the old house." It's where their nine children were born and where they all lived until recently. The old house is about double the size of Angelica's two small rooms. Its walls are constructed of bamboo poles interspersed with wood planks of varying size and topped by a scrap metal roof. In one corner firewood is stacked close to a large clay pot, which rests on three fire-charred rocks set right on the dirt floor. Nearby stand a long table, some plastic stools, and an assortment of mixing pans and dishes on a low shelf that looks as though it could double as a bench for the table.

"This is now my kitchen and where we eat," says Micaela. "Here we make the tamales and chuchitos we sell in the market. Everybody told us we make the best chuchitos for miles around, so the girls and I decided to sell them on weekends. The family has started several other small businesses along the way. When some of the kids were old enough to help Raimundo with the coffee, we saved enough to buy a goat and sell the milk. By then the littler kids wanted to have a business, too. We were growing vegetables out back so they set up a table in front of the house and sold them."

Conrad chimes in, "When I saw the kids out front selling vegetables, I was pretty sure this family was entrepreneurial. You know, I can teach people to grow and process coffee, but I don't know how to teach anybody to be an entrepreneur. You are or you aren't. Here comes Raimundo from the fields."

Raimundo's diminutive frame is made taller by his large straw hat. He is wearing the same rubber field boots as Conrad, and carrying a machete. Taking off his hat, he greets his guests who ask him to tell them about growing coffee and the history of the co-op.

"Six years ago we were selling beans to the middleman and not making much profit. That was when the eleven of us lived here in what is now the kitchen. Then some of us heard that a fellow named Conrad was teaching how to make more money from coffee. Three of us went to his classes. We liked his ideas. We talked to him about starting a cooperative and asked him to come work with us.

"One of his ideas was to rig a bicycle that separates the coffee bean from the berry. We used to do it by hand, which was a long, slow process. Now the kids hop on the bike, pedal, and have fun getting the job done.

"Can I try it? Where's the bike?" asks Carl.

"Let's go outside," says Raimundo, leading the group across the yard. Everybody laughs as Carl climbs on and pedals laboriously. Gears grind and a metal basket spins around on top where the smaller beans get separated from the berry.

As Carl winds down, Raimundo says, "Being able to sell processed beans was the first big step that brought in more money. But I've got more to tell you." Pointing to a cement-block building under some shade trees, he suggests they go to the patio of their "new house" where they've got some chairs and a roof to shade them. The slightly bigger house has enough space for the boys to have one room and the girls another. Nearby they see a young girl washing clothes in a large washstand. They can hear water and singing coming from a bamboo enclosure that must be a shower. Different sounds come from an outhouse. The multi-purpose patio houses a variety of colorful potted plants along with an assortment of chairs and tables for family gatherings. The four sewing machines in the corner are a curious addition.

The group settle themselves, and Ed leans toward Raimundo and says, "We want to hear the rest."

"When we made more money from the coffee," Raimundo continues, "the first thing Micaela and I wanted was to get all the kids to finish school

. . . at least *basico* (middle school). Then we wanted to buy some land so that we could grow more coffee. When we started the co-op, I had three *cuerdas* (roughly three-quarters of an acre). Now I have sixteen.

"My *companeros* (companions) wanted to buy more land, too. Conrad helped find some loan money to make it possible. Then he had to teach us how to keep track of it. He gave us a notebook, showed us how to write down what we got, what we spent, and what we owed. We knew we had to make a payment by the end of the year. After six months, the man who loaned the money flew down here to see if Conrad had really given it to us. We showed him the land, our notebooks, our coffee, and he was happy."

"Do I understand that the notebooks are your equivalent of an accounting system?" Ed asks Conrad.

"Yes. Each member of the co-op has a notebook. I helped them set up the first ones. I collect their notebooks monthly, review them, and combine the figures for the co-op as a whole. It's pretty simple, but it has to be."

"We learned to make money in other ways, too," adds Raimundo. "We grow our coffee under shade trees, like avocado trees, because that makes the quality of coffee better, and we can make other products. From the avocados, my son makes oil and his wife makes hand creams."

"Oh, could we try them?" ask Anabelle and Evelyn almost simultaneously.

Micaela leaves and returns with tiny jars of cream and lotion, gaining two happy new customers.

Just as some of them are silently tallying all the businesses run by this enterprising family, Raimundo tells them about one more. His older daughter, Margarita, made shoulder bags and pocketbooks from recycled coffee sacks. She stitched in zippers and colorful linings. Within two days she had sold every one. They became so popular, she got a loan to buy these treadle sewing machines you see here and hired several women from the village to help her sew the bags."

Conrad wants to make sure they understand how some well-meaning foreigners came close to ruining Margarita's business.

"The story behind this is important to outsiders who want to start a project," he tells them. "A group of do-gooders visited us. They loved Margarita's bags and bought a bunch of them. Then they went to a nearby village and decided to help them out by replicating her bags. They bought the villagers sewing machines and all the materials: the coffee sacks, the zippers, the lining, and even the thread."

Anabelle, catching on to where the story is leading, says, "Oh, dear. This must not have a happy ending."

"You're right," continues Conrad. "With no expenses, they could sell the bags at far less than Margarita's costs, which flooded the market with an unrealistically cheap product."

"So what happened when they ran out of all the materials they'd been given?"

"They'd spent everything they made; they hadn't bought any new materials and couldn't make any more bags. The good news," says Conrad with a grin, "is the market is no longer flooded. Margarita is just getting back in business."

Conrad adds, "The do-gooders are back in the U.S. and most likely have no clue how their generosity backfired on these villagers, or for that matter on Margarita. This convinces me that loans are the better way to go. For example, if the villagers had had to repay a loan, there would have been accountability. If they missed a payment, it would be a signal to find out what's wrong and do something about it."

"Okay," Stanley says, "I just want to help pay for Margarita to rebuild her business. But you're telling me loans are better. I wonder what a loan has really done for Raimundo's family? I see eleven people living in what looks like a bunkhouse with a washstand and an outhouse out back. As smart and industrious as these folks seem to be, why aren't they doing better? They deserve a flush toilet and a real stove, so Micaela doesn't have to cook in the dirt.

"You're going to tell me that I can't buy it for them, but what if I paid for a consultant to help them go further faster. Can't we get a consultant in here who will help them with a marketing plan, so they can sell to a much larger market at a higher price?"

"Stanley, we may need to hide your checkbook!" joshes Evelyn.

"You want to help everyone you meet," Anabelle chuckles. "That's the good news and the bad news."

"How about a donation for me," grins Conrad, playfully extending his palm. Carl gives him a high five and they move on.

The visitors say grateful goodbyes, and follow Conrad for two dusty blocks to another co-op member's house. Enrico meets the group at the door. His house looks like a good-sized shed similar to Raimundo's "old house." He is a slight man, wearing the same rubber boots as Conrad and Raimundo. His work pants show they have spent the morning close to the earth. He's just come home for lunch and welcomes everyone. He offers plastic stools, which they place under the macadamia tree in his dirt yard. Several chickens scurry between their feet, pecking at the ground.

"How did you come to be a member of the co-op, Enrico?" asks Carl.

"Well, I had never grown coffee before. I only picked it, working as a peon on somebody else's farm. When I saw Raimundo and the others having success with coffee, I began thinking coffee might be better for me than the corn and beans I was growing. The others in the co-op knew I was a hard worker and asked me to join. I was pleased. It is a good business and working with them sure beats working for somebody else."

Shifting on the stool, trying to conceal his backache, Carl asks, "If you haven't grown coffee before, how did you learn?"

"The ones who have experience teach the others. Raimundo and a few others began on small plots of land. I did, too. I kept my little plot of corn and beans, and rented other land for coffee. When I joined them, I copied what they were doing. They would come to check out my coffee and give me a few tips. The coffee keeps getting better. Before long I hope to be able to buy the land I'm renting.

"But what happens if someone's crop is not good quality?" asks Ed.

"Well, that happened to me my first year of production. When my *compañeros* came to look at my coffee, I had many beans that were too small. The group said, 'Your coffee is not good, we have to take it out.'" He shakes his head and sighs, "I didn't get paid for it. Now, when a new member joins the co-op, I'm the one who goes to look at my *compañero's* coffee. If it is not good, I have to take it out, the same way they did for me. That way, we make sure we're selling quality."

"Do you get paid as a group?" asks Carl.

"Oh, no. We get paid for how much we grow that's accepted. Whoever produces more good-quality beans earns more."

"But what happens if the market is flooded and the prices go down, sort of like what happened with Margarita's bags?" Ed asks with concern.

Enrico shrugs and says, "Well, I can always go back to growing corn and beans."

Conrad adds, "That's why we're developing all the other products, so he won't have to do that." Conrad moves the group on and leaves Enrico to enjoy his lunch.

In Conrad's office, they smell coffee brewing and see coffee bags piled up in the corner by a desk and filing cabinets. To the relief of Carl's aching back, there are no stools, only several over-sized chairs and a sofa. Conrad offers his guests some coffee and tells the group there is a "real bathroom" if they'd like to use it.

Even Stanley laughs, but accepts his offer and soon returns to ask his previous question. "Conrad, why don't you do this on a grander scale? This is moving at the speed of a tortoise. If you got a consultant in here, they could create a marketing plan and you could export to the U.S."

Taking a deep breath Conrad says, "Well, we're already selling to the U.S., Stanley. How much do you imagine you could grow on the small plots of land these men have?"

"Well, what if I could buy them more land?"

Putting down his coffee mug, Conrad reminds himself that these are potential donors and he needs to swallow his frustration. Someone jumping in with answers without the foggiest idea of what he's talking about drives Conrad crazy. "You are right; we've got a tortoise and not a hare. When talking about buying more land you have to remember, Stanley, it takes five years or more to enrich the soil, plant coffee seedlings, and tend them until they produce coffee. That's if the weather cooperates. You know, there are no quick fixes when you talk about growing things."

"Okay, so why not involve more men and more plots of land so more people can do better and have a real bathroom?

"I like the part about more men and more land. With more loan money available, the co-op can add men and land, and we can do just that. I hope you'll consider investing. But I'd be less than honest if I didn't point out the difference between your evaluation of "doing better" and theirs. Remember Raimundo and Enrico proudly telling you about how their earnings have increased. It has made them better off than most folks in the village. They've been able to expand their homes and their businesses, and send their kids to school. That's big! When it comes to measuring success, odds are that the co-op's annual percentage growth rate exceeds anything you've been able to do in the stock market. Incidentally, I don't know anybody here, besides us, who aspires to have a "real" bathroom.

Stanley looks a little crestfallen.

Evelyn picks up on Conrad's evaluation of the co-op's progress. "So what is the secret to all this success?"

"If I had to highlight one thing," Conrad responds, "it would be how we learn from each other and work together. We are truly consultants to each other. I've taught them how to increase coffee quality and eliminate the middleman. I've raised loan money and found markets in the States.

"But look what they do. They know their land, their climate, and how to do the most with it. They know their people and have a perfect hiring record. They've come up with simple ways to train and hold one another accountable. They keep their notebooks, and I keep the books. The farmers know some things, and I know some different things. We put together the best of what we both know and decide together," says Conrad, interlacing his fingers for emphasis.

§

The next morning the Clevelanders are on the way to their third and final visit, the reforestation project where Carl's son, Jack, had worked. They stare out the windows, drinking in this other world. Sun-drenched bougainvillea in orange, magenta, and lavender cover walls of houses alongside fields of cabbages, corn, and beans. One minute the travelers see a magnificent, postcard-perfect landscape. The next minute they are confronted with shacks perched precariously on the sides of deep ravines. Barefoot women and children carry firewood on their backs. Mangy dogs, scrawny chickens, and the occasional skinny cow roam at will. Sheep, pigs, and goats are tethered on narrow grassy strips next to the highway, dangerously close to passing traffic.

Evelyn is a little woozy with the altitude and the jostling of the van, as it winds its way up the mountain. Most of the others are conversing softly until she points out the window to wide gashes in the hillsides and gasps, "Why does it look as though somebody took a giant knife and hacked out hunks of the mountain?"

"The mudslides did that," responds Joe. "Rains from a hurricane hit up and down the country in 2008. Hundreds of people were killed. A whole village was buried alive. Six hundred thousand people lost their homes."

"Jack showed us photos of those gashes. Wasn't that what pushed him to volunteer with Save the Resources?" Stanley asks Carl.

"Yes, he wanted to help prevent mudslides like those, so he joined the reforestation effort. You can see why they need more trees. Look how steep these slopes are. Jack tells a story about a farmer with a broken leg, who when asked how he was injured answered, 'I fell off my land.'"

"I can't imagine trying to stand up on that slope. A farmer must be desperate to try to cultivate land this steep," worries Evelyn.

"But you can imagine how the forest would have looked here before. It wasn't just the mudslides that took out the trees," Joe comments. "In rural areas like this one, meals are cooked over wood fires. Three meals per day per family require a lot of trees for firewood."

"Well, they need a big tree nursery. If they don't get more trees up here soon, the rest of this land will head for the bottom," says Evelyn shaking her head.

Fredy slows the van at the sign marking "Kilometer 84," then turns off the highway and down a dirt road. Changing gears he warns, "We're in for a bumpy ride for several miles." With a wry smile he adds, "Rumor has it the money for paving this road is now a new house for the governor's mistress."

The travelers laugh but only briefly, because their attention is focused on staying upright, as the van swerves and bounces its way through deep ruts and potholes. They grip their seats and sometimes one another. "Stanley, I think I'm going to need some new dental work if we don't get there soon," Ed yells above the sounds of suitcases thumping and gears grinding.

The scent of pine permeates the van before it rolls to a stop in a little clearing by a stream. Stepping onto firm ground, the visitors inhale the cool, crisp air. Looking up, there is a dense canopy of conifers surrounding them as far as they can see. They marvel at the difference between this thickly forested mountain and the nearly barren hillsides.

Jorge is waiting for them, having heard the van. He welcomes them with a warm smile, his richly hued skin set off by his open-necked white shirt. His strong physique and confident bearing make him resemble a professional soccer player.

"I'm glad that Jack recommended you visit us. It will be my pleasure to show you around," says Jorge, extending his hand to each of them.

"Thanks, Jorge," says Carl as Joe translates, "we're so pleased to be here. Jack has told us a lot about you and Save the Resources. But until now, I couldn't imagine this forest . . . how it smells, its beauty, or how it completely blankets the mountain. It doesn't look as though you need to plant more here, but those hillsides we passed on the way could use a lot of help."

"You're right," Jorge agrees. "Ours is healthy because of how it was cared for by our ancestors. That's one reason we're growing thousands of seedlings," he says, motioning toward five greenhouses on the edge of the clearing. "The more roots that take hold of the mountain, the less likely we are to have mudslides."

A chorus of questions pours from the group faster than Joe can translate: "So why did this forest survive? Didn't they have ancestors like yours in the mudslide areas? What kind of trees? Who plants them? How many do you plant? What did the ancestors teach you?"

Noting Joe's consternation in trying to keep up, Jorge says, "We'll have time for all your questions. Would you like to sit down and continue over there?" he asks, pointing to a circle of plastic stools by the stream. The very thought of another one of those stools makes Carl's back ache. Because they are van-weary, they prefer to stand.

Clustering around Jorge, they pursue the theme of mudslides versus healthy forest. "I'm not sure about what happened with the traditions in other areas, but I do know other regions suffered much more during The

Violence. The forests were hiding places for guerillas. The military government gave land to the farmers in exchange for cutting down trees and planting crops. The guerillas went away with the forests. The land fed the farmers until the torrential rains came. They saw much of what they had worked for go down the mountain."

"But how did this forest manage to survive?" questions Evelyn still disturbed by the devastation she observed from the van.

"Well, we were never in the middle of the armed conflict, so the military didn't see the need to clear this forest. But it's our traditions that account most for why it's here. The people in the forty-eight *cantónes* (small, scattered municipal segments) around this mountain have inherited centuries of practice, working as one big community. Our fathers and grandfathers, mothers and grandmothers showed us how to care for one another, the forest, and the water sources. My grandmother used to say the caring comes with mother's milk."

"I'm curious," Ed says, "given such strong traditions and your history of caring for this lush forest yourselves, why did you need Save the Resources?"

"Ed, I think Don Antonio can answer that question better than I. He was mayor of his *cantón* during the decision to create a partnership with them. I was off at university studying environmental engineering." He smiles ruefully, "Don Antonio and the old timers tease that the university gave me amnesia, since they have to re-teach the 'city kid' the Old Ways."

Don Antonio approaches from the greenhouse, where he has been working with some school children, and takes off his straw hat to reveal a shock of white hair framing a deeply lined face. His eyes twinkle and his sun-baked wrinkles look as if they have stories to tell. There is a quality of quiet about him that seems to mirror the spirit of the mountain.

Looking at Jorge, he jokes, "I'm not sure what the *ingeniero* has been telling you, but what I can tell you is that when he came he made a lot of work for us." Jorge smiles when Don Antonio calls him "engineer." It seems to him a sign of affection, respect, and a little reminder not to take himself too seriously.

"True, Don Antonio," Jorge grins. "That's just what this group is asking about. They want to know how the forty-eight *cantónes* got involved with

Save the Resources. I told them you are the expert."

"Yes," inserts Ed. "You all have preserved this beautiful forest yourselves, so we're wondering why you need Save the Resources."

Don Antonio responds, "We've been worried because many of our children and grandchildren are losing touch with the traditions that keep the forest healthy. Save the Resources came to visit us, when we were trying to decide what to do. We didn't much like NGOs, because we don't want somebody telling us what to do. But Save the Resources is different because they work in alliances."

"Alliances?"

"We both care about protecting the forest. They were ready to support us with technical advice and some seed money. We were already organized and knew how to work together. But we had to figure out where to start."

"So what happened?"

"We had a big assembly with three representatives from each *cantón*, the way we do for all big community decisions. Save the Resources told us what kind of technical support they could provide. Then we had to decide where we needed the most help."

"So how did you decide?" asks Stanley.

"For a whole morning we listened to each other telling about animals trampling and fouling up unprotected water springs and poachers cutting down trees. Also, many of our kids and grandkids were no longer coming to the forest with us, and so they weren't learning the way we did. We named a lot of other problems, too. That's when someone suggested that we vote with beans," Don Antonio recalls.

"Did he say beans?" Ed asks.

"Yes," Joe answers, as he continues relaying Don Antonio's account.

"We set out seven baskets, one for each problem area. Each representative got three beans, which could be spread out among any three options. In no time the trees, water, and tradition baskets were the fullest. And that was the beginning of our alliance with Save the Resources.

"Soon they hired the *ingeniero* here to coordinate the work with us. We were pleased because he grew up in one of our *cantónes*, speaks our language, and knows our traditions. But we have to help him remember them sometimes. Let's take a walk in the forest, see where the seedlings are planted, and visit one of the water springs."

The well-worn path leads up a gentle slope. Sunlight filters through the branches of enormous conifers, which tower above them. The rich scent of the forest is intoxicating. Don Antonio points to smaller pines carefully spaced among tall trees, wildflowers, and assorted shrubs. Then, doing a broad jump, he demonstrates how he teaches that the seedlings must be planted "un metro" apart.

All are amazed at the sheer volume of the seedlings they see dotting the mountainside. Carl asks, "How many seedlings do you plant each year?"

"Seventy-five thousand."

"Phenomenal! How do you do it?"

"Sometimes school children and their teachers plant a few. However, most get planted by the whole community. That's when we have a big fiesta with a ceremony for the coming of the rains. We all look forward to it," says Jorge.

Ed is about to speak when Don Antonio motions them to stop and be quiet. He points high up into a fifty-foot pine, and the visitors tilt back their heads, trying to follow. "It's a quetzal," he whispers, almost reverently. "Can you see it? It has long green tail feathers and some bright red markings on its breast. They are very rare. Our ancestors tell us that the quetzal was the first bird to sing to Grandfather Sun on creation day."

Anabelle slips her hand into Stanley's and marvels in a hushed tone. "It does feel like the Garden of Eden in here."

"Maybe," says Stanley, squeezing her hand, "but I'm getting a kink in my neck."

Anabelle gives him a fond jab with her elbow as they move on with the others.

Don Antonio stops again to pick up a pinecone and extract the seeds. "See how tall and straight the tree is that grew this pinecone? These are the seeds we plant in the nursery—white pine, red pine, *pinabete, aliso,* cedar. The seeds falling from crooked trees never make it to the nursery. My father taught me how to spot the good ones; now I get to teach the younger generations."

Following the undulations of the mountain, the trail dips and rises again until they find themselves at a clear stream sprouting watercress. Several accept the offer to taste it, appreciating that it grows in one of the few streams of pure water in all of Guatemala. The sound of trickling water joins the harmonics of wind passing through the pines.

After another brief climb, they reach the *cuenca*, a cement holding tank built to capture the spring water. Protruding from it are small white plastic pipes that point downhill and go underground.

Don Antonio suggests they take a rest on a grassy carpet by the spring. Anabelle drops her backpack on the ground and sits beside it, fantasizing about how tall all those seedlings will be when their grandchildren are grown. Stanley is focused on the little white pipes, and asks, "How many people do these little pipes supply with water?"

"About two thousand, five hundred," estimates Jorge.

"You're kidding! How could they possibly meet the needs of so many people?" Mentally he counts up all the faucets in his bathrooms, kitchen, and laundry room . . . the garden hoses and sprinklers.

Carl is wondering if they have a utility company to manage this. After all, Don Antonio has explained there are twelve hundred springs all over the mountain with these little pipes serving some twenty-five thousand people in total. This is one of the most important watersheds in the whole country.

While the men discuss the intricacies of the water supply, Evelyn is absorbed in the quiet beauty of the place. Soon they hear voices from the path. It's Jorge's wife, Diana, and her committee, who have come to check the spring and clean the *cuenca*. Jorge greets Diana with a hug and introduces her to the visitors. She's petite and fits neatly under his arm. Her thick, black hair is tied back in a woven red sash.

Stanley wants to know who pays the committee for this important work. They learn that the five men and women, ranging in age from twenty-three to sixty-five, are volunteers doing their community-service assignments. It's how all the tasks get done in these *cantónes*. There are committees for everything, including dispute resolutions between spouses or neighbors, even one that hands out justice in the rare event that a crime occurs.

"This committee protects the water," Diana explains. "Protecting the water is a responsibility handed down from year to year. I take pleasure in the work because I love this mountain."

"Help me understand something," says Anabelle. "We've been hearing about the young people losing the ancestral ways. Aren't you are part of the same generation that is losing touch. What made you stay connected to your tradition?"

Jorge answers first. "As a little boy I used to walk with my grandmother to get water from a spring like this one. She showed me how to speak with the earth, the way her grandmother taught her. She had sore knees and it was not as easy for her to kneel down and give thanks as it was for me. But she did it every time, and I could see that was important. Those experiences have stayed with me and have a lot to do with my decision to spend my life preserving the forest. This is where I feel completely at home."

"It's the same for me, but also different," says Diana. In many ways it was our grandparents who helped us feel at home here. For Jorge it was his grandmother. For me it was my grandfather, who was a shaman. We would walk together here and he would give thanks to Heart of Heaven and Heart of Earth for the water, the forest, and the mountain. I spent a lot of time at my grandma and grandpa's home because my parents traveled a lot. He had a table filled with ancient stones and sacred objects. There was a place for the ceremonial fire where he would arrange flowers, light candles, and pray.

"I didn't know another way until my parents sent me to Catholic school and my 'friends' called grandfather a witch." Taking a deep breath, Diana continues, "I was very upset . . . well, confused . . . because I loved my grandfather and they made him sound so awful. He taught me that sometimes people only understand things one way. It took years of studying before I could begin to appreciate both worlds."

"Now you can see what an exceptional woman I married. She didn't tell you that besides working on the water committee, the community has recently appointed her to coordinate the work of all the water committees in the forty-eight *cantónes*. She is the youngest person and the only woman who has been given this job."

As Joe finishes translating, he looks at his watch and says, "I'm really sorry to interrupt, but we need to be heading down the mountain. We still have a long drive into the city."

As they walk through the lush forest back to the van, Evelyn remembers the bare mountainsides she saw before they came. She asks Jorge, "Will the visits from the school kids, tree planting day, and the committees be enough to keep this mountain healthy?"

"It's a slow process, but it's taking on new life. The teachers have our school children getting stories from their grandparents about the traditions they grew up with. The kids are making drawings and writing poems about the stories they've heard. Grandfathers like Don Antonio have started a program to take children on forest walks. The kids love it and he says he'd rather be in the forest with the kids than anything."

Anabelle says, "I wish I could bring my grandchildren."

§

Neon lights, horns blaring, exhaust fumes . . . what a shock to hit Guatemala City after quieter days in the mountains. Evelyn muses to herself that she is half glad to be back on more familiar ground, but already misses the people and the countryside, a different reality and a different rhythm.

At the hotel, the freshly showered visitors assemble in its dimly lit lounge. Drinks arrive as soft guitar music floats from surround sound. Carl leans back in a plush easy chair, grateful not to be perched on another plastic stool.

"That hot water felt so good," remarks Ed. "Never have I appreciated water as much as when I stepped into that shower . . . just thinking about what it takes to get clean water. How much we take for granted."

"I'm just happy I can flush it," laughs Stanley. "I don't care whether those coffee farmers want a 'real bathroom' or not. I do."

"Stanley, I think I've learned the most from you," says Evelyn. "Because each time you wanted to pay light bills or install a 'real bathroom,' it got me to question, How do any of us know when we're really doing good?"

"And that's the question for us now," interjects Carl. "The club expects us to make a recommendation. Where do you all think our donation will do the most good? Is there any danger that, like Stanley's ten thousand dollar check, it could do harm?"

After a moment of quiet Ed puts down his Coke and leans forward. "We've learned that what can hurt is when people give money without knowing what the hell they're doing or what the results will be. These three organizations value the local people, their decisions and priorities. They see the people as at least as important as the money. I'm blown away by the central role locals have in their success. It would be unlikely that some naïve, well-meaning foreigner could muck that up."

As Stanley motions to a waiter and orders some guacamole and chips, Carl continues thoughtfully, "I'm in awe of how Save the Resources and the forty-eight *cantónes* work together. With a little bit of technical help, a few volunteers from each community are providing potable water at no cost to twenty-five thousand people."

"And," interrupts Anabelle, "seventy-five thousand trees are planted by the whole community! That's amazing. And, my fourth graders would love the art program."

"Yes, agrees Carl. Besides, the reforestation project has the best shot at being self-sustaining because they rely on Save the Resources only for a small portion of the money."

"Wait a minute," says Stanley as he dips a chip in the bowl of guacamole. "Don't get carried away here. Think about Angelica and the thousands of women who can send their kids to school because of a two hundred dollar loan."

While chortling at Stanley, they all agree he has a point and order another round of drinks.

"Let's not forget the coffee co-op," inserts Ed. "Look how small loans have turned into self-sustaining businesses and how well they manage themselves."

Except for the clinking of ice and crunching of chips, there is quiet among them.

Finally, Carl breaks the silence. "My thinking has been turned upside down. I came here expecting to recommend the 'best-run' project. For me that meant how the largest number of people could be reached most efficiently. In the future, I'll look at the role of the local people and what exactly has been accomplished."

"Alright. Alright," Stanley shrugs, "I still think we have a job to help them improve their standard of living, but you have convinced me that they should have a say."

"Honey, you just need to send your money where people are asking for toilets."

"Meanwhile, we've got to make a decision," says Evelyn.

"Maybe we don't," counters Carl. "I say let's tell our club about each project, hand out some beans, and let them vote."

CHAPTER FOUR

ENSURE FEEDBACK AND ACCOUNTABILITY
Not everything that counts can be counted,
and not everything that can be counted counts

Today the air is pregnant with moisture, foretelling the coming rains. Change is in the wind.

Candelaria and Marta sit weaving in the shade of the great *pinabete* tree, which stands guard by their grandmother's front door. Their grandmother says weavings, like people, emerge from the Tree of Life.

Almost every afternoon during their school years, the two cousins came here to visit with *abuelita* and weave together. Their dreams and deepest secrets are intertwined with the bright threads. This was Marta's safe haven when her father was drinking and beat her mother. It was here that Candelaria shared the news of the scholarship that would pay for her to attend high school. Marta was glad for her, but did not share Candelaria's dream for more education. Instead, she married Eduardo. Marta had loved him since childhood. She felt sure she'd be safe in his home.

Today, chickens scurry under their backstrap looms, while *abuelita* hangs freshly dyed purple and green yarn on the line to dry. Candelaria and Marta's voices ebb and flow in a relaxed rhythm as colorful threads shuttle back and forth.

"*Gracias a Dios*, we can weave together today," says Candelaria picking up a ball of lavender yarn.

"I don't need all my fingers and toes to count when we've been able to do this in recent years. I have missed it," Marta laments. "We might not have time to weave together, but at least we have our work at MIA." The cousins started working together when the NGO, Microcredit in Action, began offering small loans in their village. Candelaria joined the staff early on. Marta was first a successful borrower, and later hired to be a loan officer like Candelaria.

As Marta pauses to watch a white butterfly land on her weaving, Candelaria teases, "Remember when you first visited Doña Beatríz, and her rickety stool sent you crashing to the floor?"

"Doña Beatríz and I still laugh at that," chuckles Marta. "Without you, my first visits to clients would have been a lot harder."

"Wait until you hear what happened this week during the women's rights class, the part about domestic violence. When I started talking about the right to be safe from personal violence, one of the younger moms began to cry. She was choked up and said that her husband beats her. He tells her that it is his right to beat her. She doesn't know what to do."

"That sounds like my mom," says Marta.

"It didn't stop there. Others admitted that their husbands beat them, too, and even beat their kids. Several women started crying, until Doña Estella stood up and said, 'The first time my husband did that, I hit him over the head with a frying pan. He hasn't hit me since.'

"That was like fireworks! We finished by talking about the legal ways to handle domestic violence, but I'm pretty sure Doña Estella's solution is the one that will stick with them."

Marta sighs, "I wish my mother had used the skillet a long time ago. I've told her about these lessons. I even said I'd go with her to bring charges against my father. She won't do it, but a couple of my clients have."

Marta continues shuttling an intricate combination of blues and greens across her loom and back. A floral pattern is slowly emerging as the weaving grows, thread by thread.

Candelaria wonders aloud, "What do you think about MIA's new growth goals?"

"It's good that many more women will get loans, but it's hard to picture what kind of changes that will bring. *Saber*" (Who knows).

§

Four North Americans from San Diego are relaxing on a rooftop terrace in Antigua, Guatemala's one time colonial capital. Janis, MIA's board president, has been here a week for a longer visit with her brother, Todd, who moved here some ten years ago. As she settles back in her recliner chair, Janis remembers how she initially complained when Todd told her he was moving. She thought it would be much too difficult to co-direct their family foundation via long distance. Instead, it's been a lifesaver. She not only got savvy about communication technology but on her frequent visits she has become a part of Antigua's expat community. During her divorce four years ago, she literally moved in for six months and tells Todd that staying with him, drinking in the view from this terrace and working with MIA, has been better and cheaper than therapy.

Doug and Randall arrived about an hour ago. Exhausted from their day of travel, they settle into their own chairs and breathe in the evening scents of geranium, jasmine, and cooking fires. It's Randall's first trip to Guatemala. He didn't expect Guatemala City's modern airport, traffic jams, or the time warp of Antigua's cobblestones and colonial architecture. Randall and Todd are old friends from prep school days. When Janis became chair of the MIA board, she began recruiting Randall in earnest to get more involved. Until now, his family foundation had exclusively funded medical research and hospitals in the San Diego area. But, Janis and Todd, with Doug's help, have finally persuaded him to consider an international philanthropic effort.

Unlike Randall, Doug is no neophyte to Guatemala. He spent his Peace Corp years here. Although he now travels the world as senior vice president in charge of human resources for a multinational corporation, he jumped at the chance to become an MIA board member when Janis asked him. After a year on the board, this will be his first opportunity to get to the countryside and see MIA's work on the ground.

As they sip drinks, Doug regales them with tales from his early years in the Peace Corps. He describes how his knees stuck out at right angles from the tiny motorcycle he rode up and down mountain trails while visiting local coffee farmers. He still remembers how they teased him with their greetings, "*Hola, Gringo Grande.*"

Randall turns to Janis, saying, "I remember when you started lobbying to get me here. I'm glad I came. I'm looking forward to seeing the project in action tomorrow and understanding more about your expansion plans. I keep wondering if growing threefold in three years will rock the boat. If I did that in my business, it would be risky."

Janis says, "You realize we've gone from zero to five thousand borrowers in five years with a continuous 99 percent repayment rate. Our branch managers and loan officers have accomplished all that. It seems to me that they've already done the hard part. Now we have their experience to build on."

"Change is always risky," says Doug, "but we are convinced we have strategies to deal with it. We know more women want loans, and the staff is eager to reach them. There are so many untapped areas, where we can repeat our model. When you meet Lucía tomorrow, she'll tell you about all the efficiencies she's identified."

"Well, it sounds like the staff is ready. But, your interest rate seems high, certainly higher than in the States. Are you ever accused of getting poor borrowers deeper in debt?"

"Yes. I had the same concern," says Todd. "It's a theme with microcredit naysayers. But the truth is MIA's interest rate is lower than anything else available to these women. They have no collateral and can only get loans from loan sharks. Along with an MIA loan, they also get the added value of trainings and the support of their borrower's group."

Doug adds, "We see the demand for loans is still strong, even when the interest is much higher than ours. We believe it is the right time to grow. Currently, our interest income doesn't cover expenses. The microfinance experts tell us to cover our overhead so our organization will be here for the long haul."

Rising slowly from his chair, Todd says, "I can't go with you tomorrow, but I'll see you off early in the morning with a thermos of coffee and some snacks for the road. For now, I'll say goodnight. It's wonderful to have all of you here, but especially you," he says to Randall, with an old-boy hug and pat on the back. Then he adds under his breath, "Let me know how much money they get out of you."

§

The next morning, Doug, Janis, and Randall follow Marta through the doorway into a borrower's home. Doug practically has to double over to get his head through the door. Janis is a little out of breath, still adapting from sea level to the highlands. She watches as Randall takes in the scene.

They enter a roomful of animated Mayan women in multi-colored *traje*. A goat bleats, two piglets tussle for a scrap of food, and a baby cries before his mother shifts him to her breast. Some women smile broadly at the visitors. Others cover their mouths, giggle, and look away. The children are wide-eyed.

Marta introduces the three strangers. They walk around the circle of women, shaking each hand and providing everyone a good laugh as they try to pronounce unfamiliar names.

Janis sees that many of the women are seated on low wooden stools, which put the women about eye-level with their toddlers. What a relief when the hostess produces "normal-sized" plastic chairs for the guests.

When the meeting begins, each client describes her business, having brought examples of her wares. In addition to animals, there is a basket of eggs, a piñata, empanadas, Christmas lights, stacks of textiles, as well as an assortment of vegetables and a mound of coffee beans.

Two of the women go to the front of the room and begin roll call. Each borrower lines up to make her payments. The women fish beneath their *huipils* and under their aprons for their secret stashes of cash. After the last payment is made, Doug thinks he'll never again look at the numbers on repayment reports the same way.

As Marta begins the training, she puts on a large, ruffled apron with two pockets and stuffs pretend money into one. Janis has seen this before and is pleased that Randall will get a picture of how MIA teaches borrowers to deal with the real challenge of separating their household money from the loan money that goes into their business. One group of women act out all the ways a new business loan can disappear when their kids, neighbors, and husbands try to get the money for something they urgently want for themselves. Another group demonstrates ways to protect the loan and make sure it goes into their business. The two groups compare how much money they have left, and why.

"This beats any power point presentation I could come up with," Randall whispers to Janis. "They're having such a good time, and it's all coming from their own experience."

As the women depart, their hostess, Doña Isabela, presents the visitors with a basket of warm empanadas. Her business is selling them to her friends and neighbors. She invites them to her back patio, where they admire the domed clay oven, which turns her dough and fillings into the acclaimed empanadas. Doña Isabela built this oven with her first loan and she plans a bigger one with her next. She'll make more empanadas and hire a couple of friends to sell them door-to-door. "*Poco a poco*" (little by little), she adds.

Randall listens to Doña Isabela telling how she now uses her profits to send two of her four children to school. As her business grows, she expects to send the other two. He's heard this called "penny capitalism." While it catches the scale of these small businesses, it has always seemed dismissive; it doesn't do Doña Isabela justice.

On the ride back into town, Randall plies Marta with questions. He knows she was among the first borrowers at MIA and has become a respected loan officer. He asks her what she did with her own first loan. Marta tells him she's a weaver and never had enough money to buy all of the thread for one weaving. Buying it in dribbles meant the threads came from different dye lots and her weavings didn't turn out as she intended. After the loan, the quality of her work was so improved that she had more customers.

Janis turns the topic to the friendships among the women. Randall has noticed the warm relationships, too, and asks, "But what happens when someone doesn't pay? Doesn't that put stress on the group?"

"It's almost the opposite," Marta explains. "We make loans to groups of women. Each member signs an agreement to pay for anyone else in the group when they can't. When someone needs to pay for a wedding, a funeral, medicine, or to feed visiting relatives, we're used to helping one another. We can count on each other."

Janis adds, "That's probably why the groups are called 'trust banks.' An additional motivation is that the whole group has to be paid up at the end of the loan cycle, or they can't get another loan. Since they have no economic collateral, this social collateral works better for us."

§

Back at the office, Randall meets Lucía, whom he's heard so much about. Janis has already told him Lucía is brilliant and the first member of her Latino family to attend college. She came to MIA with an MBA, ten years of banking experience, and another ten years managing a non-profit. She has overseen the remarkable success of this organization from the beginning.

Randall wants to know about the efficiencies she's planned. She tells him about the best practices she's researched to free up time for the loan officers to recruit and develop new borrower groups. They will reduce client meetings from two to one each month. Five-day pre-credit meetings will be streamlined to one day. Loan officers won't have to do house visits or credit checks; additional accountants will do that. A new computer system will significantly simplify reporting. Randall appreciates the way Lucía thoroughly fields all of his queries. Randall is fully engaged—the language of statistics and metrics that Lucía is using is familiar to him. He debates and encourages more discussion; a good sign for a prospective donor.

§

On a Sunday afternoon not quite a year later, light filters through the branches of their grandmother's *pinabete* tree, under which Candelaria and Marta sit weaving once again. With a *"Gracias a Dios,"* the cousins re-hitch their looms and settle into their harnesses. Threads dance back and forth.

The shared activity of weaving connects the two women to each other as surely as their looms connect them to the tree.

They exchange news about family, town gossip, and studies. As Candelaria ties off a blue thread and introduces a green one, her talk shifts to MIA. Leaning forward and releasing the pressure on her loom, Candelaria looks over to Marta, "Have you noticed any problems in your loan groups?"

Marta sighs and slows her weaving. "I'm worried because three of my best borrowers have decided to drop out and won't renew their loans next month."

"Do you know why?"

"Two of them don't like the changes. One says it's the meetings. She liked getting out of the house, visiting with the other women, and learning from the classes. Now that they just meet once a month, she doesn't feel as connected to the group. Another told me the new six-month loan isn't working for her because she raises pigs that won't be ready for market in time for her final loan payment. I need to go visit the third and find out her reasons. But God only knows when I can get there."

"I know what you mean. I can't find the time to talk with the women the way I used to. It takes me an extra hour to go to my new groups on the coast. I didn't know anybody there, so it took a long time to bring them together. I finally got my quota of three new groups, but it's like starting a new garden with no time to take care of it."

Marta agrees, "I feel the same way and I think the women feel it, too."

"What'll your group do when three members drop out?"

"The women have already said it will be difficult to trust replacements. But, I asked them to recommend new ones, who they know are reliable. They're worried that new borrowers don't have enough pre-credit training to know why they have to pay for somebody else. They're right. But, I convinced them to train the new ones themselves."

"What will happen when an all-new group has repayment problems?" asks Candelaria. I, too, worry that they don't trust one another yet."

"Yes, and there is more late-pay. Some of the women arrive late to meetings, or just send money with a neighbor or one of their children. If the borrowers stop coming, the group could fall apart."

Adjusting the tension on the loom, Candelaria pauses, trying to decide if this is the time to tell Marta. She wants her to know that, sooner or later, she'll be the one who is not coming to meetings. Her brow furrows, as she works in the new thread.

Before she can continue, Marta interjects, "When I tried to discuss re-pay problems with Gabriela, she snapped, 'Just show them the contract they signed to get the loan.' She knows many of them don't read! She doesn't sound like the woman who hired us. She's always been so supportive. She must be feeling the pressure, too." Gabriela is their branch manager, super-vised by Lucía.

Marta pauses and peers sharply at a thread that is out of place from a break in her design many rows back. She pulls on a broken thread. Chok-ing back tears, she throws up her arms and says, "Look at this mistake. I can't believe I didn't catch it sooner. It's way back at the beginning. It could take me months to undo this and reweave it . . . but I don't have any choice. It's ruining my design."

"*En serio?*" (Are you serious?) Candelaria knows the answer when she looks at Marta's face and then at the broken thread. "I'm so sorry," she says reaching over to touch Marta's hand. "I wish I could help you."

As Marta systematically begins the painstaking process of unraveling back to the break point, Candelaria picks up the conversation thread as well. "I tried to talk with Gabriela, too; I want her to know how much time it takes to chase down the women who aren't paid up. Nobody ever accused me of not working hard. But now I'm working from early mornings into the night. I can never catch my breath. I don't have enough time to study. With exams coming up, I asked to take my vacation now, and Gabriela gave me a flat, 'No,' saying we've got to keep focused on our goals. Well, I'm ready to let them focus on their goals, while I focus on mine. I think it's time I quit."

Marta gasps and then reaches over to touch Candelaria's shoulder. "I can understand. I have to admit I've considered the same thing. But my choices are different from yours. When you finish university, you will be able to get a better job. It's not the same for me. We need my paycheck to keep the kids in school."

The cousins work quietly for a few minutes. When Marta speaks up, her voice is measured.

"Candelaria, there's one other thing bothering me. You know how they keep talking about that new loan officer. It's all about Ernestina this and Ernestina that . . . all her new borrowers . . . her 100 percent repayment rate." Shaking her head, Marta says, "I don't know how she does it. But I'm tired of hearing about it."

§

Turning off her alarm, Lucía plants both feet on the tile floor of the small apartment she has rented near MIA's new central office. She stretches her arms and shivers. It has been hard to get up these cold mornings. Endless rounds of interviewing new branch managers and haggling with electricians or telephone installers have been exhausting. Nothing ever goes the way it's supposed to here. She's facing a tight timeline, so every setback looms large. When Lucía shouted at a vendor who brought the wrong chairs and then tried to convince her that his chairs were better than the ones she had expected, she realized she wasn't herself and needed a break.

Today will be different. She's going with Marta to a couple of trust bank meetings. It's always been her favorite part of the job. It will be good to see Marta and hear about Eduardo and the kids. She has watched her grow from a young borrower to one of MIA's most accomplished loan officers.

As the sun takes the chill off the early morning air, Lucía and Marta walk together to Doña Alejandra's home, only ten blocks from Marta's. Inside, twenty women and assorted children are sitting in a circle of short wooden stools. Woven sleeping mats are rolled up on the dirt floor in one corner; and in another, pots sit on the coals of the indoor cooking fire. For three years these women have been together, covering for each other's payments, learning from one another and from the trainings.

But today the women are agitated, because Doña Patricia hasn't shown up, either to make her payment or to explain why she can't. This is the second time this has occurred. After the meeting, the borrowers decide to go to her house as a group and camp out until she pays. Their spunk cheers Lucía.

As the group heads for Doña Patricia's, Marta and Lucía say their goodbyes, rushing off to the next meeting, which is one of Marta's new groups on the other side of the mountain. If all goes well, they'll be there when the meeting starts. But the bus is late, so they run up the hill. Inside the chilly, concrete municipal building, fifteen borrowers sit waiting in a circle on folding metal chairs.

As Lucía shakes hands with each, Marta greets the group president and two other women. Lucía notes the contrast between Marta's blue, green, and lavender *traje* and the red, purple, and white of the women in the group. The traditional *traje* colors of their respective villages are different, but there is more. The hugs and camaraderie among Marta, the women, and children at the last meeting are now missing. The hum of gossip and giggles is gone. Maybe it's because this is a new group, Lucía thinks.

As the president begins roll call, Marta takes the opportunity to practice matching names and faces. Two names are called that are not on Marta's list. About that time, one of the women, somewhat agitated, says, "You're telling me I have a late pay, but I paid and have my receipt right here."

Back on the bus crossing the mountain, Marta confides that today isn't the only time these discrepancies have occurred. It's upsetting to the borrowers, and Marta doesn't know what to do about it. Lucía listens, but keeps her worries to herself, hoping this is not a sign of bigger problems with the program.

§

The next morning Lucía arrives at Gabriela's two-room branch office. She's a bit late, because she didn't make connections with the bus. Commuting by chicken bus and pick-up truck until recently was a colorful adventure. Now it's slowing her down. When board members and donors come she hires a driver; now she'll probably need one all the time, she thinks.

The branch office is cozy. *Huipils* decorate the wall, and Grabriela is brewing water for instant coffee. They are scheduled to meet with Ernestina to develop a workshop to help others match her success rate. But there's no sign of Ernestina. Gabriela mentions that Ernestina hasn't shown up for several meetings recently. However, she's always called with an explanation, so maybe she's on her way.

While waiting, they sip coffee, and Lucía recounts details of her visit to the field yesterday . . . how long it took to get to the other side of the mountain and how hard it is for Marta to squeeze in all the meetings.

"Yes, all my experienced loan officers are complaining about that. So, I tell them what you've told me . . . change is always hard, but it will get easier."

Hearing the echo of her own words, Lucía says as much to herself as to Gabriela, "Yes, I'm counting on the changes getting easier. Just look at the good job your branch is doing meeting its goals."

"We have Ernestina to thank for that. Her numbers are making up for what the others aren't doing. I am hoping a few more women will soon be hitting her rate."

"Speaking of numbers, a woman was upset in Marta's new group. The record showed she had not paid, but she had her receipt. Then Marta was concerned because two borrowers were present who weren't on our master list. She says this is not the first time. Is this happening in other groups?"

Gabriela's shoulders slump. The root cause of all these problems, she thinks, is unrealistic growth goals, but decides she can't say that to Lucía.

"Gabriela, what's the matter?"

While Gabriela tries to figure out how to respond, Lucía perseveres. "We have worked together for a long time, and I've always counted on you to tell me what's really happening."

Finally, Gabriela says, "Unfortunately, I didn't know Marta was having problems. I barely have a chance to talk with the loan officers. I spend nearly all my time recruiting new ones . . . getting them and their groups set up, and doing all the reports for you and the board."

Lucía puts her hand on her shoulder, "Would it help to take a few days off?"

"Oh, no. I'd just get further behind."

Just then Lucía's cell phone rings. It's the staff auditor on his regular rounds to meet with loan officers and check their books. Lucía goes outside to get a stronger signal. Standing next to the building, she hears, "I'm here to check Ernestina's books and I'm worried. I haven't been able to track her down. So, I've gone to look for the women she reports as having loans. Half of them are nowhere to be found. It's not a good sign. We could have a case of fraud."

Lucía nearly drops the phone. Fraud? Is that possible? This is the person they're all counting on to teach the others how to be successful. Feeling light-headed, she leans against the building, takes several deep breaths, and collects herself. They discuss what they'll need to have sure proof.

As the call ends, Lucía lets herself consider the worst. How would she ever explain it to the board? Returning to Gabriela, Lucía decides to keep the suspicions secret until there's more proof.

"I'm sorry that I can't continue our conversation now, but I have an emergency and have to get back to the office right away. What you've been telling me is so important. I'll call you as soon as I can to pick up where we've left off."

Feeling very much alone, Gabriela stares at the door closing behind Lucía. She is relieved that Lucía now has an idea of what they've been going through, but she's nervous that somehow she'll be blamed.

§

For the next two weeks, Lucía visits the field in order to get a personal sense of what's going on. The news is not good. There are more problems with mismatched reports, frayed relationships with staff, and client turnover. She decides it's better to take time to understand and resolve the underlying problems now, so they can get back on track. She's increasingly convinced that will mean slowing down MIA's growth goals. The board isn't going to like it.

She places a call to Janis, who has been wonderfully supportive. What will she say about almost-certain fraud, and all the other problems? After all, Janis has raised hundreds of thousands of dollars to grow the organization.

Predictably, the first words out of Janis's mouth are, "But what will I tell investors, like Randall, who are funding the expansion? There must be another solution! Slowing down just isn't an option."

"That's what I told myself, too, but we need to take the time to understand what is going on."

As they talk, Janis tries to overcome her initial shock and calm down. Since Lucía will be returning to San Diego for the board meeting next week, they plan for her to come back a couple days early. They will work on how to present these unexpected developments to the board.

Lucía is eager to get home to San Diego, especially to her husband, Roberto. Just to be in his arms will give her strength. So will hearing him repeat his mantra, "Laugh, even though you've considered all the facts."

§

In an opulent corporate boardroom, where multi-million dollar decisions are made, nine board members have just finished dissecting Lucía's news. The polished mahogany conference table and crisp business attire stand in sharp contrast to the wooden stools, dirt floors, and moving tapestry of *huipils* in Guatemala.

Janis, Doug, and Lucía are lingering after the meeting to debrief. Doug pours himself a glass of water and leans back in the big leather chair.

"That was rough," says Janis, letting out a long, slow breath.

"But our planning paid off," Lucía says. "I was so nervous. I was afraid they'd shoot the messenger. Fortunately, you predicted they'd react the same way you did and initially focus only on investors. But, I think we worked to get the discussion beyond that."

"You kept calm," Doug says, "and it wasn't easy. I could see the treasurer tense up every time you mentioned anything that threatened the expansion."

"He wasn't the only one," Janis adds. "But when you shared the idea of creating more branches in cities to compensate for reduced numbers in rural areas, they relaxed a little."

"Even so," says Lucía, "they kept harping on finances. I don't see how we can implement new strategies without slowing down first."

"Lucía, I think you turned it around when you described your day in the field with Marta. When you asked them to picture her work and challenged them to suggest a way she could do it smarter or faster, they didn't have an answer. There's obviously a connection between eroding relationships and increased potential for fraud. It was clear they understood that Ernestina couldn't have gotten by branch managers if they were able to spend more time observing and evaluating in the field."

"I wish those human factors could show up on our spreadsheets," Doug adds. "I think a slowdown will give us the time we need to develop missing feedback measures."

"I'm glad they also saw the wisdom of paying for a consultant with cross-cultural experience like your own," Janis says to Doug. "That's just the ticket for ensuring we get the right feedback from borrowers and loan officers. I know the perfect person to evaluate the financial reporting systems. I'll see if he's available."

"Well," says Doug with relief, "it was a healthy discussion and probably a blessing in disguise. It's good we were forced to face these issues at a relatively early stage. Lucía, when you get back in the field, I want you to know that I'm only a Skype call away. Your job can be very lonely, so let's plan to talk regularly."

§

Gabriela reaches for another Alka-Seltzer. She is waiting for Lucía, who has just returned from the States. Nothing is helping her queasy stomach. Before leaving for the States, Lucía told her about the investigation into Ernestina's false reports. Gabriela has been awake every night since, worrying about being fired. After all, she feels Ernestina was her responsibility. On the other hand, it really isn't her fault. How can she possibly meet her goals without Ernestina? Maybe it's better if she loses her job. It might even be a relief.

On top of that, the loan officers are probably angry with her. They are smiling less, and she knows she's been short-tempered with them. The pressure from the board on down is taking its toll.

On entering the office, Lucía hangs up her jacket and surprises Gabriela by giving her a warm hug, the opposite of what she expected.

"I'm so glad to see you," Lucía says. "But you look worried. What is it?

Oh God, not another Ernestina."

"No. *Gracias a Dios*. Not another Ernestina. I've been losing sleep since you told me about the investigation. I feel awful. I badly needed all those new borrowers that I thought she was bringing in, and all the loans she was getting out . . . How didn't I see what was happening? And now, if the numbers aren't real, I don't know how to reach my quotas. I just don't know what to do."

"That's why I'm here. The board has agreed to give us some more time. I realize I've been so busy that I didn't sit down with you and the others and listen. I didn't go to the field until recently. Basically, I shut out any information except the numbers. What mattered, knowing the borrowers, got buried in statistics."

Gabriela begins to relax, but is still leery about what all this means. Where does it go from here?

Lucía continues, "The board wants us to take six months to understand what is going on and how to get back on solid footing. They've agreed to pay for some expert help. I've agreed to put together a small team to meet with staff and clients. We'll develop the feedback processes we've been missing. I'm hoping you and Marta will join me on that team, because you have the most experience."

Gabriela pauses and looks intently at Lucía. Slowing down is a good start, she thinks, and a relief for now. She's concerned about what will happen after the slowdown, but realizes if she joins the team, she stands a better chance of having a say.

Several days later, Marta wears her new *huipil* to meet with Lucía at the office. Lucía tells her she looks like a moving garden, as she admires each blue and lavender blossom of her intricate design.

"Marta, the first thing I want to do is thank you. When you and I went to visit your borrowers groups together, you helped me begin to understand some of what you and other loan officers have been going through. I shared with the board all you showed me, and the concerns it raised. Now I've got the board support to make some changes. I'm hoping you'll join Gabriela and me in figuring out what is working and what's not.

Marta wonders if this really means they want to know about everything that's falling apart. The problems are very much alive. Only last week a good friend in another branch told her that their loan officers were talking about going on strike. They have a manager who yells at them for not signing up enough borrowers. The manager falsely accused her friend of exaggerating travel expenses and then refused reimbursement. Speaking slowly, Marta says. "I'd like to see things change, and I'd like to help that happen. But this would be very difficult. I just don't have any more time in my day."

Lucía assures Marta she would find someone to cover her loan groups. Marta's fingers absently tuck a fold of her *huipil* into her woven belt as she hears Lucía saying to her, "You're right that it won't be easy to go back and get to the bottom of the issues."

Marta's fingers pass over the area she rewove. She remembers the broken threads and the hours to unravel and reweave them. But going back to the mistake had given her an inspiration. The blue flowers she started with are now combined with a variety of lavender ones, and touches of metallic thread infuse the flowers with light. She likes the new design, even though it took four extra months to do it. As Marta hears the first drops of the rainy season patter on the office roof, she decides to join the team. She knows it will be difficult, but maybe MIA will weave something better, once they get back to the broken threads.

CHAPTER FIVE

EVALUATE EVERY STEP OF THE WAY
What you see depends on where you stand.

With each circle of the wooden spoon, around and around in the batter, Stephanie feels herself releasing tension as she stirs. Here in her small Guatemalan kitchen, she is baking her grandmother's favorite chocolate cake. Her grandmother was a tenacious woman. Stephanie feels the strength of her resolve as she assembles the familiar ingredients.

She can hear her grandma's voice saying, "The way to the heart is through the stomach!" Stephanie gently folds the flour mixture into the moist ingredients. If sharing this cake with the *curanderas* (healers) from the cooperative can inspire even a little bit of connection, maybe she and the women can begin to make some headway. After months of meetings, Stephanie has tried everything she can think of to get their business started. Now she is trying cake.

Being here in Guatemala is so important to her. Not only does it fulfill a childhood dream to experience places and people who look and live differently from her, it is also a part of her career plan.

She'd had an epiphany when she watched a documentary about impoverished women who were turning microloans into successful businesses in Bangladesh and all over the world. At the time, Stephanie had been finishing her MBA in International Economics and an internship with a multinational corporation. But, the film suddenly made clear to her that nearly all of her training and experience had been from the perspective of the "West," not the "Rest." Her professors often would say, "The world is getting smaller by the minute," yet the Bangladeshi women's experiences could not be further from her own.

So here she is in her second year working with a small stipend for an NGO in Guatemala that placed her with a group of women, mostly grand-mothers, called *curanderas*. They grow herbs, make them into tradition-al medicines, prescribe, and sell them to the local people. After forming a cooperative, her NGO decided to help them develop another business so they could increase their income. Given their expertise with herbs, the NGO determined it made sense for them to make and sell herbal soaps, shampoos, and lotions. Stephanie accepted the job, because it sounded like a perfect opportunity to apply her international economics training in a developing country. The NGO promised she would have supervision during her two-year stint. That hasn't happened; and neither soaps nor lo-tions have been produced.

Stephanie has felt isolated. Skype conversations with friends and fami-ly have been her lifeline. On the other hand, they don't seem to know where Guatemala is, saying "Honey, we hope you're happy in 'Guadalajara . . . or is it 'Guadalupe?'"

New gringo friends in the city also lift her spirits. With them she can get a break and do a little partying on weekends. They go to restaurants that offer more than beans and tortillas, stroll the shopping malls, and go out dancing. They are living and working in urban situations and tend to give her advice, which bears no resemblance to the realities of her life or those of Indigenous people in the rural highlands. They're teaching junior achievement classes to city kids, and she's working with herbs and grand-mas in the countryside.

For months she has been casting about for tactics that would get the *curanderas* to care about soap. Stephanie was cooking when inspiration arrived in the form of a C.S. Lewis quote, "What you see and hear depends on where you stand." "That's it!" she had exclaimed. She'd been trying to get the *curanderas* to listen to her, but maybe she had been standing too far away to understand what they were telling her. She resolved to get closer—and bring cake with her.

§

Stephanie slowly pours the batter into a baking dish and sets it in the warm oven. As she closes the oven door, she's grateful she has one of the few "real" stoves in the village. She thinks back to her first meeting at the cooperative. The secretary at the NGO had told her the time and the place. She had put on her best blouse and nervously rehearsed what she'd say, checking a few words in her Spanish dictionary. Walking several blocks to the co-op, she had been filled with anticipation.

She remembers approaching the small wooden building, really a shack with herb gardens surrounding it. When knocking on the door elicited no response, Stephanie turned the handle and found herself in a room furnished only with three wooden benches, a short table, and a cupboard full of small bottles. These were painstakingly labeled, but with words that were not yet in her vocabulary.

Where are the curanderas? she wondered. *Is this the right date?* As long minutes stretched into an hour, and then an hour and a half, anxiety turned to frustration. The longer Stephanie waited, the more she worried whether there had been a misunderstanding, or worse, were the women deliberately avoiding meeting her? She had been told that Guatemalans are often late, but this much? She wondered if being a New Yorker made her congenitally incapable of waiting around. She gave it fifteen more minutes before heading back to the NGO offices.

The only staff person had been the secretary, because the director was in the States raising money. Consequently, she received the brunt of Stephanie's annoyance. Stephanie asked for a contact among the *curanderas* to find out when the next meeting would be. The secretary regretfully shook her head. She was apologetic, but offered little advice other than to try again next week.

§

The sweet smell of baking chocolate draws Stephanie's attention back to the kitchen. She picks up the near-empty mixing bowl. With two fingers she licks it clean before taking the bowl to the *pila*. The *pila*! Now there's another thing she hadn't known about when she arrived.

She knew the *pila* was where she was supposed to wash. But what was it doing out back? And how was she supposed to use its three strange compartments? She had watched her pile of dirty laundry grow and her supply of clean socks and underwear diminish. She longed for a washing machine. When she had stretched the limits of her wardrobe, she resolved to visit the public *pila*, where women gather to wash and share the day's gossip. Perhaps she could learn from them how to use it.

As a foreigner, Stephanie was a novelty at the communal *pila*. Chatter and scrubbing were briefly suspended as the women eyed her and her bulging bag of laundry. She remembers shifting uneasily from one foot to the other, her laundry protruding in front of her as though awaiting a midwife.

Nervously, she tried to determine what to do with the multiple sink compartments. She spied a supply of unattended water and tossed her dirty clothes into the large basin with a splash. Several women looked aghast and others put their wet hands over their mouths to cover their giggles, which echoed off the tin roof overhead. Stephanie wondered what she had done.

After an agonizing minute, the woman next to her said, "Would you like me to show you how it works?" As Stephanie nodded, she leaned over and picked up an item from her own wash, and said, "The clean water comes from the middle."

With a sinking feeling, Stephanie realized she had contaminated the source of clean water for the whole communal *pila*. A woman at the next sink cast a scathing glance in her direction and Stephanie stammered an apology. Her rescuer comforted her with her matter-of-fact tone. "Water is precious, especially in the dry season, so we use as little as possible. I'm glad to teach you," she continued, demonstrating with her wash. Stephanie copied her every action.

"Thank you for being such a patient teacher."

"Actually, I am a teacher, but my regular students are in the fourth grade. My name is Elena and it was my pleasure to give you laundry lessons," Elena grinned. "Are you here for long? What country are you from?"

As they chatted and became acquainted, Stephanie had savored every word from this warm and outgoing woman. Once Elena had departed with her clean wash, Stephanie found herself hoping that they might meet again.

Stephanie's return trips to the *pila* had renewed her energy for tackling other things she didn't know, which generally meant life in Guatemala and specifically anything to do with *curanderas* and herbs. She was apprehensive as she went to their next scheduled meeting, but to her relief the shack was full of women. She remembers her mind was spinning, scrambling the names of the women with the names of the herbs. The *curanderas* would pinch off leaves from different plants, crush them with their fingers, and hold them up to Stephanie's nose for her to inhale their fragrance. They seemed to be telling her about the plant's medicinal purposes, but Stephanie was imagining which ones might be best for soaps and lotions. When she began discussing the new business venture, she was met with strangely blank expressions.

She finally got up the courage to ask the president of the group, Doña Celestina, when they could start production. "You are experts with plants. The NGO knows this will be a good business for you." Then it was Doña Celestina who looked confused. She explained that it was true they know a lot about herbs, but they did not want to make soap. They wanted the NGO to help them to raise chickens and sell eggs. When Stephanie asked Doña Celestina if she had told the director that, the answer was, "Oh, no. He didn't ask."

So, she realized, the job she had been hired to do wasn't something the community had agreed to. But soap was the plan the NGO was ready to fund. Stephanie knew how to push ahead (wasn't that what New Yorkers are born to do?). She started a campaign to convince the women.

She was pleased with all the ingenuity and creativity she had poured into touting the benefits of herbal products. She had made cost and return ratios come alive with brightly colored charts and pictures of tourists. She used live chickens, chicken feed, eggs, and a skit simulating sales to demonstrate the higher cost of raising chickens compared to the potential profit from herbal products. A friend from the city came and told them exactly how a group of women had started a successful soap business in a nearby village.

The women had been amused, but not persuaded. They said they understood they'd make less with chickens. But Doña Inez explained, "Chickens and eggs always sell in the market, and on slow days we can always find hungry mouths at home happy to eat whatever doesn't sell." Stephanie slowly understood there was more motivating the women than a "bottom line."

§

Stephanie realized she needed to focus more on the community, even if it was hard to miss her gringo friends. Staying home was lonely at first, until one day she met Elena, the schoolteacher from the *pila*. They decided to go for a lemonade. Elena was coughing and complaining that all the colds and runny noses of her fourth graders had finally reached her, too. Stephanie asked her what kind of medicine she was taking. Elena replied that her mother is a *curandera* and always fixes her sore throats with *te de limón*. Stephanie did a double take and put down her lemonade.

"What is your mother's name?" she asked.

"Celestina Upan Bajan," Elena responded.

"Is she a member of the *curandera* cooperative?"

"Yes. She's the president."

"That's the co-op where I've been working. How come we didn't make the connection before?"

"Mamá said there was a gringa working there. I wondered if it was you," Elena says, coughing.

"I appreciate the special way she has with the other *curanderas*. I'd love to have a cup of her *te de limón* sometime."

Only a few days later, Elena invited Stephanie to the home where she lives with her mother, father, and extended family. Relaxed at the kitchen table, they sipped a fragrant, steaming cup of Doña Celestina's tea. As they chatted, Stephanie told Celestina about her first day at the cooperative, when she waited several hours for the meeting that never materialized.

Celestina smiled and explained that it must have been the day when the priest was in town for his monthly visit . . . which always includes all the weddings, baptisms, and funerals that stack up in-between times. As usual, most of the *curanderas* had probably been at church.

Stephanie remembers being jarred by this news. She'd been here almost a year, yet still didn't realize this monthly ritual occurred. It reinforced her decision to stay in the village on weekends.

§

Sniffing the air, Stephanie's nose tells her the cake is ready. Lifting it carefully from the oven, she places it on a rack to cool and begins mixing the icing.

When Stephanie walks to the cooperative holding the plate, she feels the familiar anticipation that heralded any event featuring this cake back home . . . birthdays, graduations, baby showers. She walks in, and heads turn. Labeling herbal tinctures stops. Embroidery is set aside. Conversations hang in midair. When a grinning Ana Maria pronounces, "It's a fiesta!" one member slips out to the garden and brings back some mint for garnish. Another picks flowers to put beside it and another makes herbal tea. Within minutes, the party is in full swing.

Sitting down beside Celestina, Stephanie tells her it was her grandma's favorite recipe.

"There were no cakes like this when I was young," Celestina says. "Until recently, we made everything from corn, because that's what grows best here. I think you know we are Tz'utujil, but you might not know that *Tz'utujil* means 'the people who come from the corn flower.' Our food, our corn, is at the heart of who we are. Instead of sweet cake at times of celebration, my grandmother made tamales that everyone in town hoped to taste."

"Mmm . . . I like tamales."

"Yes, we've noticed! You honor us by eating our food. Many gringos are afraid to try it or don't like it. How can they understand us if they don't eat the corn that makes us who we are."

"What made your grandmother's tamales special? Could I learn how to make them? Or is her recipe a family secret?"

Celestina didn't answer immediately, but after several moments responds, "I'd like to teach you, Stephanie. Elena and the rest of the family will be very pleased, because normally I make them only for Christmas and Easter. You'll need to come early, and we probably won't finish until dark."

Stephanie beams. "That would be wonderful! When would you like to do it?"

"How about next Saturday?" Celestina quickly shakes her head, "Oh, of course that won't work because you go away."

"No, no," Stephanie interjects hastily, "I have been thinking that I would like to stay here on weekends. It would be a wonderful gift to help prepare the corn with you and share tamales with your family. Saturday would be perfect."

Some of the women overhearing this conversation offer to teach her their specialties, until one says, "Slow down. She can't even make tortillas yet!"

"You're right," Stephanie laughs. "But I do know how to eat them! I've heard that gringos can't ever make tortillas right. It's just not in our genes. But I'd love to try."

Several of the women volunteer to help her.

"You just want to see me make a fool of myself one more time!" she teases them.

§

When Stephanie enters Celestina's kitchen, she sees a pile of cornhusks soaking in a wide basin. Dried corn is waiting by a well-worn *metate* (grinding stone) and *mano* (its roller), which Celestina explains came from her grandmother.

"It is a part of my *abuela's* recipe. You just don't get the same flavor with the new *metates*," she insists.

No wonder these women are so strong, Stephanie thinks, an hour or so later, as she struggles to keep grinding. It may resemble a rolling pin but, as Stephanie quickly discovers, the stone *mano* is many times heavier. She tries not to let on that her arms are killing her, but Celestina notices and puts her to work stirring the sauces, which has a few special touches:

a pinch of oregano, some ground *pepitas* (pumpkin seeds), and a dash of *canela* (cinnamon). As they grind and stir and line up cornhusks, they exchange more family stories. When Celestina talks about how her *abuela* read the moon and stars to know when to plant the corn, Stephanie recalls her own grandma, who grew up on a farm in Nebraska, telling her exactly the same thing.

Feeling their familiarity growing, Stephanie risks asking, "Celestina, I'm wondering if you could help me understand why you and the other *curanderas* want to sell eggs, when there's not much money in it. They have explained that the chickens and eggs are easier to sell in the market, but there must be more to it than that."

Celestina, who has had her own frustrations in these exchanges about chickens and soaps, pauses . . . then asks, "Who would buy expensive soap?"

"Remember those tourists in the photos that I showed you? They were spending a lot of money."

"Yes, but we don't go to that market. It's too far away and we don't know people there. Tourists seldom come here. Even if they did, we could not depend on them. They might go somewhere else or stop coming. Chickens and eggs are what we understand. We buy and sell chickens and eggs from one another every day right here. I've never sold anything to a foreigner; I don't understand them, or they, me."

"Now, that I understand!" exclaims Stephanie. "It's like me at the *pila*."

Elena, who's walking through the door, laughs. Chuckling, the three of them decide to take a break for some tea.

"You've learned a lot since that day," Elena offers.

Celestina nods in agreement, as she pours the tea.

"And I have a long way to go," Stephanie sighs. "So, here is my problem. The NGO will give you funding to make soap. What do you think it will take for the *curanderas* to get comfortable enough to take advantage of this opportunity? Or at least to know what they're giving up?"

"We need to know where we will find the tourists," says Celestina.

"None of us have sold anything to foreigners before," adds Elena. "And how do you make fancy soap anyway? We know how to make laundry soap, but tourist soaps must be different."

Celestina asks Stephanie and Elena to go to the courtyard to bring her a little more fresh oregano for the sauce. Celestina's five grandchildren are playing tag in the bright sunlight under the clothesline. Stephanie admires the many flowering plants and herbs. She asks Elena about the separate little enclosures surrounding the courtyard, and learns that as each of her brothers married, her father, Roberto, the village carpenter, built them separate rooms.

Stephanie sees one wall made of white canvas stamped with the huge letters "USAID." When she asks, Elena explains that it is a leftover from the emergency shelters the United States erected for the survivors of the mudslides a couple of years ago. Other walls are made of bamboo, adobe, corrugated metal, and wood planks painted bright colors.

Roberto's carpenter shop is in the corner of the courtyard closest to the entryway, with its own door off the street. It seems to be a gathering place for the men of the village. But the kitchen with its long wooden table is clearly the heart of the home. Stephanie and Elena return with a small bundle of oregano and are offered a fresh cup of mint tea. The red pork sauce and green chicken sauce bubble on the big wood stove, aromas wafting through the kitchen and beyond. She watches with pleasure as an assortment of neighbors wander in and out, tasting the sauces and gossiping.

Lying in her bed that night with a full stomach, Stephanie feels the satisfying exhaustion that comes from a rich, full day. As she rubs her muscles, sore from grinding corn, she realizes what a heady type she is. That has served her well in schools and internships, but this situation requires something else. All the strategies she imported to persuade the *curanderas* are good on paper, but got her nowhere before sharing cake and tamales.

Until this morning, she didn't understand much about the significance of corn to this community. What is it she still doesn't understand about the chickens? Celestina talks about chickens as part of the fabric of their lives . . . almost as important as corn. Stephanie begins to wonder for the first time if she needs to pay more attention to chickens than soap.

Celestina's words gnaw at her. "What would happen if the tourists don't come?" It's true the locals will always eat eggs. So, perhaps the women would make less money, but would they have less risk? She knows that tourist traffic fluctuates as a result of everything from intimidating articles about Guatemala in U.S. newspapers to global economic downturns. *Maybe these women know better*, Stephanie thinks. She resolves to meet with the NGO director to discuss this, whether he wants to or not.

Earlier this morning, she was convinced she would win the *curanderas* over to her way. But now, as she turns off the lights, her thoughts shift to winning over the NGO director to the women's point of view. She's caught in the middle.

In the NGO office the next morning, Stephanie feels fortunate to find the director behind his desk instead of out raising money or checking on projects. He looks up from his papers, and says, "Well, good morning, Stephanie. This is a pleasant surprise. How's the soap and lotion business going?"

"Well, frankly it's not going anywhere. I know you brought me here for that . . . and I've been working really hard to make it happen. I can tell you everything that I've done, but more importantly, I came to tell you that these women never wanted a soap and lotion business. They want to raise chickens and sell eggs."

The director frowns and Stephanie presses on. "After a full year, they've finally told me how they feel and what they want. So, I came here to ask you what you think about helping them start a chicken business instead?"

The director is baffled. "That doesn't make any sense. These women work in herbs. They are experts in herbs!"

"I know. I had the same reaction. The truth is, they don't use fancy soaps, and have never sold to tourists, who seldom come here anyway. As one of them said to me, 'We understand eggs. We buy eggs from one another every day. We eat eggs. We don't eat soap.'"

"Don't they understand that we're here to help them? Haven't you told them that they can make a lot more money from soaps and lotions than from chickens?"

"Believe me, I've tried." Then she has him laughing aloud telling him about bringing in live chickens to one of their meetings. Stephanie adds, "But the president of the cooperative, who is a wise woman, has pointed out that selling soaps to tourists is a very risky business."

"Right. I think I get the *curandera's* point. But chickens are a risky business too. They get diseases and die all the time. Besides, what it boils down to is that our organization is about entrepreneurism. It's how I raise money. Our donors want to support those who will begin new businesses. There are already plenty of chickens here, but there is no soap business. This donor has funded a soap business in Africa and now wants to do it here. I seriously doubt he'll give money for chickens rather than soap, and I don't want to turn away a donor who is willing to provide this opportunity. Look, if you keep working with the women to do herbal soaps, I'll look for another donor to fund chickens."

§

At the next co-op meeting, the women can't wait to hear how Stephanie did with making tamales. When they ask Celestina, she pantomimes Stephanie hunched over the grinding stone. Then she praises Stephanie, reporting that it took her only a few tries before catching on to the trick of assembling the dough securely within its cornhusk wrapper, so that the sauce stayed inside throughout the steaming. Stephanie says she now understands why Celestina's grandmother's tamales are famous.

"Thanks to Celestina, I not only know something about making tamales, but she helped me understand why every time I talk about soap, you want to talk about chickens. Is it true that most of you don't want to go to the market in the city?"

In the chorus of relieved responses, Stephanie hears: " . . . the trip is too long . . . it costs too much . . . I can't take time from my family . . . what if I'm not here when someone needs my herbs to get well . . . we don't know anyone in the city . . . tourists don't speak our language."

"I think I finally get it," Stephanie says. "But I'm wondering if there might be places where tourists pass through nearer here?"

Ana Maria, Celestina's close friend, suggests tentatively, "My aunt sells textiles outside the restaurant up on the highway. All the tourist buses stop there."

Some of the women look at each other, as though this might be an idea worth exploring. Several others sit in the corner with their arms folded, as though daring the group to even consider it.

"Who would like to go with Stephanie and me up to the bus stop to see what it's like?" Celestina asks. "This doesn't necessarily mean we'll do anything with soap, but it can't hurt to go see. Who knows, maybe we could sell eggs there, too." Hands go up with volunteers to make the trip.

At the next meeting, reporting back from their bus-stop excursion, the women are brimming with new information. "Tourists climbed out of five different buses during the two hours we were outside the restaurant," they explain, all talking at once. "After they eat and go to the bathroom, the tourists don't have anything to do but shop. We looked at all the things being sold, from fruit to blankets."

"We watched the women selling to travelers," adds Ana Maria. "They don't all speak Spanish. But, I saw the visitors playing with the sellers' children. Some take the tourists to their mothers' stall, where the visitors buy and take pictures."

Another *curandera* adds, "I was nervous about telling someone prices, because I don't speak their language. But it wasn't a problem, because they didn't have to say a word. The seller just added up the cost on a little calculator and showed it to the customer."

After more questions and answers, Celestina says to the group, "So, after hearing this, what do you think?"

"I don't know . . . I just can't imagine making soap."

"Me either. And I don't want to go up to the bus stop and sell to strangers all day."

"Well, I felt that way, too," says Ana Maria, "until I saw that we could really make money there. Maybe the rest of you should go up to the bus stop and see. The other thing is I'm getting nervous about chickens. My cousin raises them. He came by last night. He was really worried because some of his chickens are sick. They are not eating and several have died. He reminded me that he's had this problem before."

"Oh no. Some of my sister's chickens are dying too," adds another *curandera*.

Stephanie thinks that she doesn't wish ill for the chickens or their owners. But she's happy that at least some of the *curanderas* can see the risks.

"Well, even so, I just like having them running around. We've always had chickens."

"How do you make fancy soap anyway?"

Celestina interjects, "There's something else we need to think about. Where would we get the money to get into the chicken business? We know that the NGO has promised to pay for making soap, not chickens. I suggest that we try making soap, so we know firsthand what it takes, and then we can decide whether we want to continue. Are you interested?" She sees most of the women nodding yes, so she asks, "Who wants to come over to my kitchen?" Stephanie feels a rush of excitement as the women begin to take ownership of the project.

They measure and mix the ingredients, putting them in small molds made from cutting tin cans in half. It takes several more days in Celestina's kitchen and many tries. At first the soap is runny. Then it has air bubbles. Getting the right proportion of herbs for the scent they want is also tricky. So it goes, until they get it right. When they give out samples to all the co-op members, Ana jokes that they need to be careful using the new soaps because the fragrances they've added are so powerful that their husbands will be chasing them.

§

Stephanie can't wait to share this breakthrough with her family. She sits down to write an e-mail. As she has immersed herself in village life, her communications back home slowed. "And so," she writes, "after months of going in more circles than I can count, chocolate cake, tamales, dead chickens, and a soap lab, we are ready to launch a full-fledged business. We experimented and experimented until we got something that looks like soap, feels like soap, and smells like soap. It washes and makes suds.

"Most of the women are into it now. There are still a few on the edge of the group who don't like the idea and want to undermine the project. Celestina tells me not to worry. It's hard for some people to accept change. Well, we all know people who are like that. Thank God for Celestina, she's got my back."

She finishes that e-mail with, "Stay tuned. I'll be taking your orders soon."

At the next co-op meeting the soap business takes a new turn. Who would have thought that picking colors for the packaging would be such a hassle. The *curanderas* want packages and labels in the bright colors of their textiles, while Stephanie's marketing research suggests that currently tourists are more attracted to earth tones. But the *curanderas* are adamant, so Stephanie suggests that they make packages of both the bright and the natural colors and take them to the bus stop to find out what people buy.

When the earth tone packages fly off the sales table, the *curanderas* change their minds. Stephanie resists the impulse to point out that she was right. In their growing enthusiasm for the business they no longer think of it as her idea. Their ownership of the project increases Stephanie's optimism that the business can now grow without her.

Finally, it looks as though the soap project may really get going. The donor and the NGO director will be pleased. He hasn't yet found money for chickens. But, who knows, maybe the women will use their earnings to start a chicken business, too.

With her two-year job contract nearing its end, Stephanie's beginning to feel she's accomplished something. She had thought she would never be able to make a change here, but now realizes the biggest change has been her own.

§

Exiting the subway at 79th Street, Stephanie wraps her red chenille scarf tighter about her neck, against the frosty December air. While navigating the crowded sidewalks, she clutches her briefcase in one hand and a bag of warm bagels in the other. Her high heels meet the concrete in hasty, spine-jarring strides, provoking a memory of walking the village path in sandals, kicking up puffs of warm earth and carrying cake to the *curanderas*.

The fast pace of New York's competitive world of smart phones and meetings, her schedule packed from early morning workouts to late-night parties, has always seemed exhilarating. Often it still is. But in the more frenzied moments of office deadlines, she finds herself longing for a leisurely cup of tea with Celestina. She even misses talk of chickens. Culture shock in both directions continually surprises her.

As an executive assistant, she's learned much of the best of "the West." Stephanie is up on technology, budgets, and product distribution. She's become a pro at juggling the details of her bosses' schedules and heading off conflicts with other departments. It's just that the other departments don't slow down and talk with one another. The departmental silos have conflicting priorities as they focus on their particular goals. Stephanie wants them to start by seeing the customers' needs as their common objective, what's best for "the rest."

For months she has been building relationships with her counterparts in other departments. At long last they have agreed to an early morning meeting to discuss the customer's viewpoint. With bagels to share in hand, and cake with the *curanderas* in mind, she heads for the conference room.

CONCLUSION

We Have Done It Ourselves

Go to the people:
Live with them. Learn from them.
Love them.
Start with what they know.
Build with what they have.
But the best leaders,
when the job is done,
the task accomplished,
the people will say:
We have done it ourselves.
—Lao Tzu

Lao Tzu's wisdom encapsulates the themes in *Doing Good*, but his advice is hard to follow. The hundreds of people who inspired the stories in this book know that truth. They told us about the myriad of unexpected complications they met when attempting to "do good." They shared their small and large epiphanies. People with good intentions, including us, don't have all the answers. But, we believe success comes when "outsiders" partner with local people in the many steps toward achieving mutually agreed-upon goals . . . so the people can say, "We have done it ourselves."

The question at the heart of this book is: How does doing good become *We have done it ourselves*? The themes of our five chapters emerge as guiding principles. Each is a part of every success story. They are like five threads that can be woven in various combinations, colors, and textures.

1. Respect and value the people.
2. Build trust through relationships.
3. Do "with" rather than "for."
4. Ensure feedback and accountability.
5. Evaluate every step of the way.

These principles help intended beneficiaries have a real say in deciding and implementing outcomes. In chapter three, Conrad makes the point. "The farmers know some things, and I know some different things. We put together the best of what we both know and decide together."

He reminds us of a stove project we once heard about. A long-term volunteer with a technological bent was living in a Salvadoran village. He became concerned about the amount of scarce firewood being used for traditional indoor cooking fires. The smoke was also making families sick. He studied up on the various kinds of fuel-efficient stoves and began to build one in his front yard. Each day a friendly neighbor walking by on her way to the market would stop and they'd talk about his progress. One day she pointed out that the fire was too close to the ground, and no woman would want to bend down so low to stir her beans. Another morning she mentioned that the surface was too small to cook tortillas for the whole family. A few days later she told him he should put a space in the front for warming a pot of beans. After weeks of alterations, she finally agreed that it was a good stove and asked him to build one inside her home. The volunteer had heard that some stoves given to people in nearby villages were being used as flowerpots. So he agreed to construct one for her out of simple, low-cost materials, if she would show him how to get her neighbors to use them. They made the stove together. Then she showed her friends and they built more of them. As the new stoves became popular in the village, the people could say, "We've done it ourselves."

As you'll recall from the Introduction of this book, a doctor and chief spent time together . . . even liked each other, yet could not agree to build latrines for the village. What was the difference? The doctor came from a culture where no one would question the value of latrines. For the chief, however, latrines were a foreign concept and not part of his experience.

This is quite a different situation from the volunteer and his Salvadoran neighbor who shared an understanding about the value of stoves; so they worked together to improve them. But, what happens when foreigners and local people can't grasp each others' goals?

Our beliefs and assumptions are deeply ingrained in us, many of them unconscious. They color how we view the world. They can get in the way of understanding and fully engaging those we hope to help. So, how can we see beyond our own experience?

Ivan Ilich says we can't, at least not in a few weeks. In his now-classic 1968 speech, "To Hell With Good Intentions," he challenged a group of students off to do service projects in Mexico: "By definition, you cannot help being ultimately vacationing salesman for the middle class 'American way of life,' since that is really the only life you know . . . I am here to challenge you to recognize your inability, your powerlessness, and your incapacity to do the good which you intended to do. Come to look, come to climb our mountains, to enjoy our flowers. Come to study. But do not come to help."

Certainly in working on this book, our own assumptions have been challenged repeatedly. When we met the individual who became Amalia in chapter one, her limited education and her lack of "our kind" of critical thinking clouded our view of her. That changed the day she told us about the tourists on the boat taking her picture. She wondered aloud what they could know about Cristobal and herself from their photos. She was even more curious about who they were, what they were thinking, why they seemed nervous, or if they had suffered in the past. Her curiosity, her thoughtful questioning, and the way her own traumas informed her thinking, all made us look again.

Looking more closely, with deeper respect, is the first principle for doing good.

RESPECT AND VALUE THE PEOPLE

What do you picture when you think someone is "poor?" The World Bank did a survey of more than sixty thousand people in sixty low-income nations, asking: "What is poverty?" Corbett and Fickkert[3] repeated the survey with middle-to-upper-class churchgoers in North America. They gave very different answers. The people living in poverty spoke of the effects it had on their dignity as persons . . . causing fear, shame, humiliation, inferiority, hopelessness, depression, powerlessness, voicelessness, and social isolation. The wealthier North Americans more often named poverty as a lack of material things, such as food, clothing, housing, clean water, money, and medicine. In our interviews we heard from Guatemalan locals who described how badly they felt when somebody called them poor. They didn't think of themselves as poor.

In chapter one, Amalia says, "We're not less because we have less." Diane wants Ellie to see the person before seeing the poverty—as a subject not an object. As subjects, people have a say. As objects, they don't. In the Kaqchikel and Tz'utujil languages, no one can "be poor" because there is no verb "to be." Instead, identity is in belonging to the family, the sun, the forest, and the corn in a web of exchange. One might come from a humble family, but they can't "be poor." However, in English or Spanish when we say someone "is poor," we don't separate the person from the poverty. In this way of looking at the situation, respect and value for the individual can disappear.

Larry Dressler, author of *Standing in the Fire*, offers his way of respecting the people without ignoring poverty.

> "Over the past seven years working in Guatemala . . . I have stumbled upon a spiritual practice that I call 'holding two truths.' You don't have to spend a lot of time in places like Guatemala to discover two very different narratives. One truth is about 'the beauty'—the exquisite natural landscape, colorful culture, and the resourceful, openhearted people, and the possibilities. The other

---

3 Corbett, Steve, and Brian Fikkert. *When Helping Hurts: How to Alleviate Poverty without Hurting the Poor—and Yourself.* Chicago, IL: Moody Publishers, 2009.

truth is the brokenness—the disturbing and self-perpetuating cycles of poverty, illiteracy, corruption, and violence. The trap is that on any given day it's easy to get caught in seeing the place and our work through just one of these lenses. I might think, 'this place is hopelessly broken and needs our organization to help them 'fix it' or 'Yeah, these people are poor and hungry but look at how happy they are with their colorful culture and optimistic nature.' When we get caught up in only one of these narratives we become vulnerable to doing our work in ways that cause more suffering.

"When we get caught up only in the 'beauty' narrative we romanticize the people and place and deny the hard facts on the ground. When we focus only on the 'brokenness' narrative we are susceptible to becoming mired in hopelessness or adopting the stance of a rescuer. Learning to hold two contradictory truths simultaneously is the uncomfortable and necessary work each of us must do to dance well with the complexity on the ground. The work of holding two truths enhances our capacity to respect and value the people in and beyond the context in which we first see them."

A waitress holds one truth about a little girl's order in a restaurant and another truth about her parents' order. They all meet in a story retold by Tara Brach[4] about a family who went out to dinner. When the waitress arrived, the parents gave their orders. The five-year-old daughter piped up with her own: "I'll have a hot dog, French fries, and a Coke!" "Oh, no you won't," interjected her dad, and turning to the waitress he said, "She'll have meat loaf, mashed potatoes, and milk." Looking at the child with a smile, the waitress said, "So, honey, what do you want on your hot dog?" When she left, the parents sat stunned and silent. But, the little girl, eyes shining, said, "She thinks I'm real."

---

4 Brach, Tara. *Radical Acceptance: Embracing Your Life with the Heart of a Buddha,* New York: Bantam Books, 2004.

What does it take for the person you're trying to help to say honestly, "She thinks I'm real?"

BUILD TRUST THROUGH RELATIONSHIPS

Who do you trust—and why? In chapter two, Lucy knew the people wouldn't come just because the clinic opened its doors. She listened and learned, hiring people widely respected in the community. *Promotores* (health promoters) built more relationships of trust in the community by taking health care and education into the homes of their neighbors.

The person who became "Lucy" was originally introduced to health promoters in graduate school, where she read about Paul Farmer's work in Haiti and around the world. Even with limited resources, Farmer has been able to expand medical support dramatically by training teams of health promoters, whom he calls *accompagnateurs* (accompaniers).[5] They visit homes, doing preventive health care and follow-up with patients. He says it's been an effective strategy in Boston as well as developing countries, because *accompagnateurs* have been able to help patients with a variety of needs beyond immediate medical treatment. For example, they help them stay on schedule with appointments and medications, and assist in dealing with problems like childcare and paying the rent.

That was the kind of partnership that Chenta, the clinic nurse, had with Eduardo and his family. Their trust in her made it possible for them to overcome their fear and for Eduardo to have life-saving surgery. "Accompaniment is different from aid," Farmer says. "Aid connotes a short-term, one-way encounter: one person helps and another is helped. Accompaniment seeks to abandon the temporal and directional nature of aid; it implies an open-ended commitment to another, a partnership in the deepest sense of the word."[6] Where relationships build trust, the capacity to help multiplies.

---

5 In Latin America the term "accompaniers" more often refers to human rights workers, who shield people named as "subversives" by military death squads.

6 Farmer, Paul. *To Repair the World: Paul Farmer Speaks to the Next Generation*, ed. Jonathan Weigel, California Series in Public Anthropology (California: University of California Press, 2013), Kindle 292–98.

In chapter five, Stephanie couldn't understand why the *curanderas* wouldn't talk to her about the soap business she was hired to start. It wasn't until she gave up weekend partying with friends in the city and decided to focus on life in the village that she began to build relationships. Doing her laundry at the communal washstand allowed her to learn from the women she was there to help. Soap and water, tamales, and cake became the ingredients of reciprocal exchanges, which slowly built trust with Elena and Celestina, and eventually with most of the *curanderas*. As Robert Lupton says in his book, *Toxic Charity*,[7] "It is delicate work, . . . establishing authentic parity between people of unequal power. But relationships built on reciprocal exchange . . . make this possible."

Relationships are best carefully built over months—but even a thirty-minute relational meeting can make a difference. In the Greater Boston Interfaith Organization (GBIO), people from nearly every racial, ethnic, religious, and socio-economic group come together, amassing significant political power. Relational meetings, "one to ones," build their shared foundation of understanding and trust.

It can work like magic, as it did when a conservative synagogue offered to host a large gathering in their space. Several days before the event, the synagogue learned that the executive director of the Islamic Cultural Center would be chairing the meeting. The rabbi asked GBIO to replace him, worried how some synagogue members would react. The GBIO said it would move the venue, if necessary, but it wouldn't replace the Muslim director as chairperson. The GBIO organizer suggested that a few relational meetings be arranged quickly between the Jewish synagogue members and the Muslim center members. In these face-to-face meetings, they shared the similar injustices their parents and grandparents had experienced as immigrants in sweatshops and ghettos. That changed their relationship and the meeting went on as planned. When the Muslim director announced that fifty members of his congregation would participate in the next political action, it was members of the synagogue who led a standing ovation.

---

7 Lupton, Robert D. *Toxic Charity: How Churches and Charities Hurt Those They Help (and How to Reverse It)*, Harper One, 2011.

As Atul Gawande writes, "Human interaction is the key force in over-coming resistance and speeding change."[8]

DO "WITH" RATHER THAN "FOR"

How would you want to get help, if you needed it? The group from Cleveland had their eyes opened by the three successful collaborative projects they visited . . . and how much was accomplished. It may be easier to give handouts, but even Stanley began to see the difference between working "with" the people and doing things "for" them.

In crisis situations like floods, hurricanes, tornadoes, and all manner of natural disasters, doing "for" can be a necessary and worthy response. Doing "for" in situations of chronic, institutionalized poverty is more likely to promote dependency, marked by one-way relationships between givers and receivers, sometimes seen as rescuers and victims. For example, when U.S. churches "channel enormous amounts of material resources into global mission, sometimes in ways that make the control of money . . . the primary determinant of decision making and power,"[9] they risk creating significant inequities. A different kind of Golden Rule can ensue: the ones with the gold make the rules.

In *Toxic Charity*[10], Robert Lupton illustrates how "doing for" can be changed into "doing with" by relating an experience at the home of his neighbor on Christmas Eve. In their impoverished section of the inner city, the children excitedly waited for the folks from a suburban church to arrive with gifts. When the doorbell rang, Lupton watched the father, looking ashamed, slip out the back door. That moment propelled Lupton to create a Christmas store at a local church, where the generous suburban parishioners could bring their gifts. Parents would come, select and purchase the gifts for their children at favorable prices, then wrap and deliver them themselves.

---

8 Gawande, Atul. "Slow Ideas," *The New Yorker,* July 29, 2013, p. 42.

9 Priest, Robert J., Douglas Wilson and Adelle Johnson, *U.S. Megachurches and New Patterns of Global Mission.* (Report); An article from: *International Bulletin,* May 2010.

10 Lupton, Robert D., Ibid.

The two of us started this book with a bias against doing "for," or what some call the charity model. Connie's perspective on doing "for" shifted when she was volunteering as translator for Spanish-speaking clients at her church's food pantry. In the 1980s, small streams of Central American refugees were beginning to show up at U.S. food banks and homeless shelters with life-and-death stories of fleeing from war and violence. In a long line of Latina mothers with lots of kids, stood a tall, muscular young man. He told Connie he was AWOL from his post as a sergeant in the Honduran military. When she asked how and why he was there, he reported, "One day, I went home on leave to visit my mother. She was very poor and I had joined the army so my pay could help her. But she took me to the secret place in her kitchen where she had hidden her life savings. She stuffed it all into my hands, saying, 'You have to leave here because the army has you killing your brothers and sisters.'" At that point Connie decided that handing out food might attend to a passing need, but didn't address the deeper root causes of hunger and violence. She shifted to human rights work.

Early in life, Fran tasted the insult that sometimes comes when we try to "do good." A church group started giving her first-grade friend their old clothes. Fran wondered why, because she and her friend dressed quite alike in clothes hand sewn by their moms. Her friend may have lived in poverty, but she didn't need or want this "gift." She would never wear those clothes. This memory continues to make Fran sensitive to when "doing for" isn't "doing good."

Peter Buffet cautions his fellow philanthropists that charity in the form of handouts is potentially "philanthropic colonialism." It makes the giver feel better but keeps "the existing structure of inequality in place."[11]

Unequal power relationships are built into Guatemala's history. The Spanish conquest in the sixteenth century decimated the Mayans of Guatemala, enslaved them, and appropriated the land they had cultivated for more than three thousand years . . . all with the ecclesial blessing of the

---

11 Buffet, Peter. "Op Ed: The Charitable-Industrial Complex," *New York Times*, July 26, 2013.

Pope.[12] That reality is reflected today in every social, economic, religious, political, and military aspect of Guatemalan society. It has played out most recently in the thirty-six years of "civil war," "the violence," "armed-conflict," or "genocide."

Reflecting on that prolonged violence, Tani Adams[13] asks, "What happens to human beings when it becomes 'normal' everyday life to live with high levels of violence?" Her research concludes, "when we live in chronic violence, parents are unable to nurture their children adequately; social relations become more restricted, polarized, and conflictive; and our role as citizens or participants in the larger community suffers."

The history of violence constitutes an intrinsic challenge when establishing equal power relationships "with" partners to achieve mutually agreed-upon outcomes.

ENSURE FEEDBACK AND ACCOUNTABILITY

How do you define success? How do you know if you're succeeding? Meaningful measurement often finishes last among an NGO's competing priorities. With tight budgets and staff more passionate about program activity than statistics, doing research and bean counting can, understandably, take a back seat.

This is especially true for informal organizations, like the church group that started the coffee-bag sewing project in chapter three. When they saw the purses the *campesino's* daughter made, they assumed their copycat idea would bring the same success in another village. They went home, proud of their work, and never found out that it had become a failure—even causing some harm. By neglecting to evaluate outcomes, caring people sometimes make it look as though they don't care.

---

12 In the Papal Bull of 1452, also known as the Doctrine of Discovery, the Pope sanctioned the Christian enslavement and power over non-Christians "to capture, vanquish, perpetually enslave [them, and] take all their possessions and their property."

13 Adams, Tani. "Chronic Violence and its Reproduction: Perverse Trends in Social Relations, Citizenship, and Democracy in Latin America," Woodrow Wilson International Center for Scholars, 2011. http//www.woodrowilsoncenter.org

In *The White Man's Burden*, William Easterly[14] points out that lack of feedback and accountability are the most critical flaws in existing aid. The person who became "Marta" in chapter four would agree. Had she, Candelaria, and the women in their loan groups been listened to, the outcomes for them and MIA (Microcredit in Action) could have gotten back on track sooner. The irony was that in an organization built on solidarity, trust was undermined. As Robert Lupton says, "Accountability reinforces trust."[15] When all parties are "doing with" one another from the outset, the chances of getting reliable feedback and having useful measures are improved. How can you trust someone to tell you if an effort is failing, if you haven't trusted them from the outset to define success?

Dean Karlan and Jacob Appel[16] give us another slant on getting reliable feedback in *More Than Good Intentions*. By researching under what conditions local people will and won't use a water purifier, they determined what would work. They tell about a town in Kenya where 70 percent of the people knew that dirty drinking water causes diarrhea. Almost 90 percent had heard about a chlorine solution that would purify water and reduce the diarrhea substantially. It had been distributed in many villages and was being sold in their local stores, but very few put it in their water. A variety of tactics were tested. Some that seemed obvious turned out not to be very effective, or not for long. The most successful was a dispenser installed at the town faucet, the only water source. It released exactly the amount of chlorine needed to purify the typical twenty-liter jerry can of water. You could fill it and let it mix as you walked home with it on your head. This approach led to sustained behavior change. Usage continued to increase for months and remained high even a year and a half later. The people voted with their feet.

Along with unused chlorine solutions, we've seen stoves used as flow-

---

14 Easterly, William. *The White Man's Burden: Why the West Efforts to Aid the Rest Have Done So Much Ill and So Little Good* (New York: The Penguin Press, 2006).

15 Lupton, Robert D., Ibid.

16 Karlan, Dean and Jacob Appel, *More Than Good Intentions: Improving the Ways the World's Poor Borrow, Save, Farm, Learn, and Stay Healthy* (New York: Dutton Adult, 2011).

erpots and nutrition supplements sold for pig feed. What's forgotten is that very few of us do what others say is good for us. After all, how many, including the two of us, exercise and eat the way the doctor tells us to? Change comes hard. Resisting it is human nature. In any volunteer project, objective and practical analysis of what works and what doesn't is essential to make sure investments of both time and money are well spent.

How to measure desired outcomes isn't always obvious. A doctor we interviewed pointed out that some NGOs tout the number of meals served or calories consumed as the measure of a successful nutrition program. But that doesn't make any difference unless the children's health is improved. A few NGOs do measure children's weight, but he says the most reliable indicator is height.

Much has been written about the fact that over the past two decades, trillions of dollars and millions of hours have been directed to aid for poverty alleviation worldwide with little impact. William Easterly and Robert Lupton lead a chorus of voices saying that unexamined consequences are at the heart of the problem. We found that to be true in many organizations formal and informal, large and small. As Karlan and Appel say, "If a development program is supposed to help solve a specific, concrete problem, let's put it to a specific concrete test . . . if it passes, great . . . if not, fix it or try something else."[17]

EVALUATE EVERY STEP OF THE WAY

Stephanie went round and round with the *curanderas* in chapter five. When one thing didn't work she tried another, just as though Paulo Freire were whispering his praxis model in her ear. "Knowledge emerges only through continuous inquiry, invention, and reinvention."[18] Once the *curanderas* agreed to try making and selling soaps, together they tested a series of new ideas with more members of the cooperative contributing to the changes at each turn.

---

17 Karlan, Dean and Jacob Appel, Ibid.

18 Freire, Paulo. *Pedagogy of the Oppressed,* 30th Anniversary ed. (New York: Continuum, 2002).

The action and reflection process is a way of life in the Greater Boston Interfaith Organization (GBIO); members of its congregations identify the issues they care about most in their community. At meetings in
Haitian churches, nursing-home workers shared stories about how they
were required to work under conditions unsafe for them and their patients. They were being assigned many more than the recommended
number of patients, making it physically impossible to care for them all.
Describing painful details of a culture of disrespect, they explained that
they were not allowed to speak Creole in their break room. Sometimes
they would be called into work, but not needed, and sent home without
pay. That reflection process propelled a series of actions, reflections, and
revised actions.

As a result of meetings with families of patients, nursing-home managers, and the Attorney General's office, a GBIO leadership team developed
a Patient and Worker's Bill of Rights for nursing homes to sign. When that
strategy failed, the team invented other actions. Finally, at a meeting of
several hundred GBIO members, the Attorney General agreed to an un-
precedented Advisory to the Nursing Home Industry, clarifying the civil
rights of nursing-home workers. Mandatory training sessions for industry
leaders regarding how to properly protect these rights on a daily basis fol-
lowed. It was a real victory for the workers, who reported they were now
being treated better, and thus were better able to care for their patients.

In the praxis model, evaluating every step of the way is essential. Continuing reflection helps identify changing circumstances, how to learn
from failure, and better ways to accomplish goals.

As authors, we have lived the cycles of action and reflection in writing
this book, as six years of waste paper baskets and document "deletes" would
attest. For example, when we wrote and rewrote about Save the Resources'
reforestation project in the third chapter, it kept going flat. Finally, we realized that most of what we were recycling only came from interviews with
the man who became "Jorge." We decided we needed to better understand
the context, so we traveled to the mountain he told us about. There, Jorge
introduced us to "Don Antonio," "Diana," and others. When we heard their
voices and walked through that vibrant forest, the story came alive. We

rewrote the section several more times and reflected again with Jorge, until he authenticated what remains here.

The process of trial and error is a good teacher.

DOING GOOD IN A WEEK OR TWO

How much good can you do in a few days? The degree to which individuals can implement any of the five principles depends largely on how much time they have, what skills they bring, and how well those skills are fitted to desired outcomes in any given situation. It's not possible to embody the wisdom of Lao Tzu and build the kind of relationships he suggests in a week or two. However, of the approximately one million people who volunteer internationally each year, 45 percent, or 450,000 people, did so for two weeks or less. While data is limited, it appears that a high percentage of those were on mission trips.[19]

The first challenge for all short-termers is to develop reasonable expectations. Being useful may boil down simply to listening and learning. If all a volunteer does is begin to understand and appreciate the people and their culture, there's a good chance of a mutually valuable experience.

Here's what some NGO staff have to report. These vignettes are not meant to discourage short-termers but rather to help them ask the question: "How can I be more useful?" One staffer, who directs the efforts of more than 2,000 one-to-two week missioners each year, said:

"We make a point of calling them 'visitors' rather than volunteers. We pick them up at the airport, house and feed them, and transport them to worksites. We train them how to do jobs they haven't done before. We supervise them, hold their hands, and hand out medicine when they get too much sun or brush their teeth with tap water.

---

19 Lough, Benjamin J. *International Volunteering from the United States between 2004 and 2012.* Washington University in St. Louis. Research brief, 2013. CSD publication #13–14.

"They cost us more than the value of any work they can do in the time they're here. Many are constantly frustrated because they think we're not keeping them busy enough. When building materials aren't delivered to a site on time, what are we supposed to do? A couple of times we've resorted to having the complainers move rocks across the road. On the other hand, their visits are good for fundraising over time. They get their churches involved and generations of parishioners contribute and come to visit. Some visitors tell us they've become more caring about people living in poverty and more appreciative of how lucky they are. We do know that a handful of them get the bug and come back for a year or two."

What do you envision leaving behind as a volunteer? It might feel good to build someone a home—but does it always "do good?" The burgeoning number of volunteers building houses prompted the founder of an NGO to comment, "It's tangible. They can touch it, see it, photo it, and feel they've done something important. What they don't realize is that they're taking jobs away from the local people who typically know more than the volunteers do about building and could do it a lot cheaper."

Debate continues over the cost of travel and care of short-term missioners building houses. Is it better for them to come or just send the money and get the work done locally? A study done by Kurt Ver Beek[20] evaluated a project, which built houses in Honduras following a devastating hurricane. Estimated expenses for volunteer travel, food, and lodging meant that each house they built cost $30,000. The identical house built by local labor cost $2,000. Fourteen more houses could have been added with the money spent for the one house built by the missioners. The same researcher also tracked whether the volunteers' world-view or actions were changed by the experience. They discovered that within six-to-eight weeks after the trip, there was little in the way of lasting changes, either in giving

20 Ver Beek, Kurt Alan. "The Impact of Short-Term Missions: A Case Study of House Construction in Honduras After Hurricane Mitch," *Missiology*, 34, no. 4 (October, 2006) 477–495.

for mission or attitudes toward others. "The sheer fact of encounter with cultural difference is as likely to increase ethnocentrism as decrease it."[21]

Small NGOs have unique considerations. Language students, retirees, and individual travelers arrive unannounced, hoping to help out for a while. But smaller NGOs can't usually afford a volunteer coordinator to tend to questions or do the hours of training needed. Generally, do-gooders "who parachute in" distract staff from their full-time jobs, especially when they don't speak the local language.

The bilingual and bicultural Guatemalan director of a clinic that serves several villages says she can only use a few volunteers. She selects them very carefully, because her primary focus is on the clinic's relationship with the community, rather than the volunteers. She personally trains and supervises new arrivals until she's sure they won't accidentally undermine the clinic's credibility in the villages. With the two or three volunteers she selects to work with school kids in the clinic's hygiene and nutrition program, she actually does a week of role-play, anticipating what the kids might do or say. For the volunteer doctors and medical students she selects, she insists that a Guatemalan medical staff member accompany them during every patient interaction.

"I don't care how much medical knowledge they have," she says. "There are cultural differences they couldn't possibly pick up on. Also, Spanish is not the first language for either the volunteer or the patient. Some of them balk at my dress code, too, but what they wear and how they behave reflects on the clinic. Flip-flops, tank tops, and skirts above the knee are not appropriate . . . and speaking English excludes everybody but the gringos. It's not allowed. Oh, and absolutely no picture taking . . . and . . . Pa.a.a.l.ease, I tell them, don't talk about the U.S. lifestyle. When you compare the food or houses you're used to, people here think you're saying they're not as good, even if that's not what you meant. And what-

---

21 Priest, Robert J., Terry Dischinger, Steve Rasmussen, C. M. Brownet. "Researching the Short-term Mission Movement." Research paper, p. 444. www.academia.edu.

ever you do, don't start talking about all the poverty you've seen during your week in the countryside. This may be an adventure for you, but it's people's lives here. You have a passport and a charge card. You can always fly home. That's a choice they don't have."

Nearly all the volunteer coordinators and NGO staffs we interviewed asked us to tell readers: "Make sure you're doing something the NGO wants done and that you have the skills to do it. Come prepared. Read about the country and culture. Follow the guidelines you're given, and above all, respect the people. We appreciate those who show up on time, take their tasks seriously, do the work cheerfully, and don't disappear if they find something better to do. If you don't speak Spanish you may find you're needed doing data entry, working in a library, teaching English, or planting trees. If you're building things or playing with children, be sure to hook up with a well-supervised program."

The founder of an NGO told us about her "star" volunteer. "She was fluent in Spanish . . . really fluent, not just thinking she was because she studied it in school. She had experience working with young children and was a self-starter. She talked to people in the village, spent time with them, and realized they wanted and needed something for the kids to do when they got out of school. So she started reading to some kids in the afternoon. She checked in with the director regularly, to keep her posted and to make sure she was doing what was needed. She was so good, we convinced her to stay and develop an afterschool program."

§

Some of you reading this book will have already done volunteer work at home or abroad. Others may be about to take their first trip and are feeling the excitement and anticipation of venturing into another culture. Don't lose that enthusiasm—but go in with the five guiding principles firmly in hand. We hope they will serve you as a kind of GPS system for richer and more productive experiences of *Doing Good* with those you meet.

Respect and value the people.
Build trust through relationships.
Do "with" rather than "for."
Ensure feedback and accountability.
Evaluate every step of the way.

We are grateful to the many people who helped us understand what doing good looks like from their vantage points. The short-termers and long-termers, donors and board members, staffers and NGO founders, and, especially, the receivers of their efforts have shown us the complexity of turning good intentions into productive outcomes. We hope the experience you've had reading this book has provoked your thinking and will inform your decisions and actions for *Doing Good*. Please share your own experiences on our blog at www.doinggoodsayswho.com. There are no easy answers, but our ongoing questions and reflections can keep the learning alive.

DISCUSSION GUIDE

The questions that follow are designed to facilitate personal and group reflection. We suggest using them before, during, and after engaging in projects aimed at doing good. Are you going with a group? Meet up with your travel team the month before—or if you need, at the airport during the first (second, third) layover, and break out this book. Pick a facilitator, choose a couple of questions that will help you open to new experiences, and get ready to question your assumptions. While you're experiencing another culture, dig deeper into the questions. When you get home, see if your answers have changed.

Some readers may prefer a limited menu of questions, but we are too fond of options. So we highlight one or two queries per section for those with less time, and offer more for further conversation. Choose what works for you.

DOING GOOD . . . SAYS WHO?

6. Think about a time when you had a personal experience of someone doing good for you. What worked? What didn't? What were your feelings?

7. Think of a time when you experienced doing good for others. What worked? What didn't? Do you know if they saw it the same way?

8. Have you ever "gone outside your comfort zone" into another culture? What happened and what did you learn?

9. When an aboriginal elder, Lilla Watson, said: "If you have come to help me, you are wasting your time. If your liberation is bound

up with mine, let us work together." What does that mean? (Do an internet search for "Lilla Watson.")

10. What picture comes into your mind when you hear the word "poverty?"

11. When middle-class people in U.S. churches were asked to define poverty, they described a lack of food, clothing, and housing. When people living in poverty were asked the same question, they named lack of choice, isolation, shame, depression, and powerlessness. Why do you think there is this difference in perception—and how might it affect efforts to do good?

12. There is a saying, "history is traditionally written by the victors." When entering a new culture—or examining your own as an outsider might see it—how do you get the whole picture?

13. Pick any chapter and discuss: Who has the resources/power? What kind of resources/power do they have? Who decides how the resources will be used? Who benefits from the decisions? What are the short- and long-term consequences?

14. How can you know whether you and local people agree on the changes to be made?

15. What are you missing when you look only at needs rather than assets?

16. What is meant by "failure can be a good thing?" Identify some significant failures of well-meaning efforts in the book. What was learned? When have you learned from failures in your life?

17. How could the guiding principles of *Doing Good* apply for you at home as well as abroad?

QUESTIONS BY CHAPTER

Chapter One. Respect and Value the People

1. What does Amalia mean when she says, "We're not less because we have less?"

2. Have you ever experienced seeing poverty before seeing the person? Have personally experienced being pre-judged? What happened—how were relationships and collaboration affected?

3. What are the differences in how Amalia, Diane, and Ellie deal with the stolen toilet? What works—and what doesn't?

4. What does Larry Dressler mean when he says we need to practice "holding two truths?" What is a situation in your life where you've "held two truths?"

5. What motivates the different characters in this chapter? With whom do you most identify, personally?

Chapter Two. Build Trust Through Relationships

1. Have you ever moved to an unfamiliar place? How did you get to know your neighbors and their beliefs?

2. What steps does Lucy take to build relationships in the clinic's community?

3. What different ways do short- and long-term volunteers help the clinic and community?

4. What do *promotoras* add to the delivery of health care? How can outsiders help the work of *promotoras*?

5. What are your views on family planning? Would the women at the river agree with you?

6. If you wanted to join a medical mission team, what would you look for?

7. Was there anyone in this chapter who helped you see something from a different perspective? Who? What?

Chapter Three: Do "With" Rather Than "For"

1. What are common characteristics in the three projects that make them successful?

2. Stanley asks, "Why is it so damn complicated to help someone out?" Is there a bit of Stanley's attitude in all of us? Where does it come from? When can it be useful? Is it harmful?

3. If Joe and Fredy weren't guiding the group, what might the visitors miss?

4. When a local woman tells Joe not to make beggars of her children, what did she mean?

5. How does the North American solution-oriented, fix-it, make it bigger-and-better culture play out in this chapter?

6. If sustainability is a priority, what difference does it make when doing "with" or doing "for"?

Chapter Four. Ensure Feedback and Accountability

1. What does *Not everything that counts can be counted, and not everything that can be counted counts* mean?"

2. For whom does the NGO exist? The institution? Recipients of services? Donors? Boards? Are accountability and impact measurements different for each?

3. How did MIA measure the change it wanted? What else did they need to know? Describe a situation that you knew was deteriorating, but the people in charge didn't see it.

4. Why are front-line staff often left out of the development of measurement tools? How is their input important?

5. We know that implicit power and cultural norms often compel local people to give responses that please the asker. How might you get reliable feedback?

6. The human factor "isn't reported on spreadsheets." How can social impact be counted as well as economic effects?

7. What role does social collateral (group payback) have in the functioning of trust banks? How is it measured?

8. How does an NGO decide when industry "best practices" are right for them, or not?

9. How does an NGO decide if bigger is better? If better, what are the criteria for managing the growth?

Chapter Five. Evaluate Every Step of the Way

1. "Evaluate every step of the way" means repeating cycles of action and reflection—also called "praxis." How does Stephanie act and reflect? How does it help her?

2. How does Stephanie learn from failure?

3. What did it take for the *curanderas* and Stephanie to build a relationship?

4. How could a short-term volunteer work to do the same?

5. How much say should donors have in driving mission?

6. Is Stephanie different for her experience? How might it influence her career in international business?

Conclusion: Getting to "We Have Done It Ourselves"

1. Peter Buffet says that charity (in the form of handouts) can keep existing structures of inequality in place. How? Is that true in your experience?

2. Atul Gawande says relationships are key "to overcoming resistance and speeding change." Has this been true in your life, work, and attempts at "doing good?"

3. Why is questioning our assumptions an important ingredient in "doing good?"

4. When are short-term volunteers most valuable?

5. What is the motivation behind your good intentions? What does it feel like to consider that your actions might not be as helpful as you hoped?

6. What is the most important insight about doing good that you have recognized in reading this book?

APPENDIX

Doing Good ... Says Who? poses a question. Who gets to say what doing good means? In researching the answers (and there are many), we undertook an iterative process. We reached out to Guatemalans, students, NGOs, mission groups, and others. We asked about their experiences, listening and probing further.

This book intends to fill the gap between academic research and "how to" prescriptions. We describe experiences of working across cultures through narrative to provoke discussion and challenge assumptions. In this appendix, we share our process in order to be transparent about how the narratives are constructed—and encourage others to take up our work where we leave off. More research is needed; more stories are ready to be told.

RESEARCH DESIGN

Doing Good is primarily based on qualitative research with individuals and group participants in over four hundred and thirty formal and informal interviews. The interviews took place over five years, from 2009 to 2014.

The purpose of our research was twofold: First, to find out what kind of experiences and relationships Guatemalans have with the variety of foreigners who come into their culture to do good; and second, to understand the viewpoints of both Guatemalans and foreigners about what "doing good" means to them. We used a variety of qualitative research techniques to gather and record the experiences and diverse perspectives of interviewees.

SAMPLE SELECTION PROCESS

As a first step, we listed categories of Guatemalans and outsiders to be interviewed. We wanted representatives of the cultural, economic, educational, and political diversity among Maya and *ladino* (non-Maya) Guatemalans. Similarly, we listed foreigners coming from various generational, economic, social, political, non-religious, and religious backgrounds. The latter included non-denominational evangelicals, Catholics, Presbyterians, Methodists, Mennonites, Quakers, and Anglicans.

The next step was to identify people we knew with whom mutual trust already existed. Additionally, we researched NGOs, found contacts in each, and requested interviews. None of them turned us down. In every interview we asked for referrals and recommendations to further contacts with similar as well as opposing or alternative viewpoints.

1) Interview Candidates

Most interviews were done with individuals. Some were selected for in-depth, multiple interviews, because their experience provided more comprehensive details than others from the same criterion sampling cohort. A few Indigenous individuals were interviewed repeatedly to provide critical feedback on our representation of Maya realities.

The group interviews included Maya clients of several NGOs and, in one case, the all-Maya board of directors. We personally conducted most of the interviews, but we also trained and provided a list of questions to bilingual Maya and Spanish speakers who interviewed individuals and groups in their shared language and reported back to us in Spanish.

We conducted interviews in cities, towns, villages, and hamlets in the Guatemalan highlands, most within a sixty-mile radius of Antigua, Quetzaltenango, and Lake Atitlán.

2) Interview Content

All interviews began with the interviewer explaining the project, promising the interviewee(s) anonymity, and answering their questions. The interviews consisted of open-ended questions with substantial follow-up questions designed to plumb the respondent's experience, feelings, and perspective. We asked Guatemalans to tell us about their experiences with volunteers and NGOs, what they saw as the positive and/or negative aspects of those interactions, and what they wished foreigners knew. We asked foreigners to tell us about their motivation for coming, about their experiences with Guatemalans, the positives and/or negatives of those interactions, what they learned, and how they were different for the experience.

3) Interview Statistics

Overall our database contains four hundred and thirty responses, 52 percent of which come from Guatemalans. One hundred and eighty-four people participated in individual interviews. Of those, we did more than three in-depth interviews with thirty-five of them, and eight of those participated in five to ten intensity interviews, shadowing and/or reviewing and critiquing cultural content. Group interviews involved one hundred and thirty-nine individuals. Additionally, we estimate at least a hundred informal dialogues with people in our personal networks, and they shared relevant experiences. Approximately seventy-five individuals from a wide variety of perspectives have read and critiqued all or part of our writing along the way.

The majority of interviews were recorded and transcribed, some handwritten in notebooks. These original documents are stored. Some unrecorded discussions—and, of course, our lifetimes of informal discussions and relationships in Guatemala—also informed the stories we tell in this book.

CHOOSING A NARRATIVE

During the early years of interviewing, we began organizing the hundreds of vignettes on index cards. We sorted and resorted the cards by topics, by types of volunteers, types of projects, and a variety of other combinations. What evolved was akin to a collection of static snapshots in a scrapbook, rather than the dynamic interactions respondents reported.

The challenge was to merge multiple voices into a coherent whole, which would bring the interviews to life while maintaining their integrity.

"Fictionalizing" in controlled ways offered several advantages. Important-ly, the anonymity we promised would be assured. Material from a variety of interviews could be turned into dialogue by editing quotes from inter-views to make them fit into the context of the story. Also, we could com-bine interviews from a target group like donors and present their views and experience in one character, reflecting composite details from many donor respondents. By placing characters from different cultures with varying values and perspectives in relationship in the same scene or context, we were able to show the tensions and misunderstandings, as well as similari-ties, they told us about.

Paramount was to keep the meaning and spirit of what interviewees told us. The key characters in each chapter have read (or had read to them in their language) their story. Each has verified that we have represented the meaning and spirit of what they told us and that they found nothing misleading.

We recognize that fictionalizing these stories is problematic. There is a risk that we may not have portrayed their stories accurately. Readers should keep in mind that any representation of another person's story is biased by who is telling it. We have constructed these narratives with as much com-mitment to accuracy as we are able, recognizing that we may not have fully portrayed individuals the way they might have represented themselves. In the long run we decided that fictionalizing was a risk worth taking.

METHODOLOGY BY CHAPTER

Chapter One

The main protagonists, "Amalia" and "Diane," are the product of intensity sampling, so called for the multiple in-depth interviews with each of them in their homes, in our homes, shadowing Amalia on the job, and several years of close relationships with them both. While each of their stories is unique, it should also be noted that at their core they are representative of the experience of many more people. For example, the descriptions of Amalia's family, her schooling, and her "kidnapping" were told to us similarly by many other Guatemalans. Likewise, Diane's founding of an NGO, her struggle to understand the culture, her relationships with students and staff, and the ongoing task of raising money are struggles shared by many other NGO founders we interviewed.

"Ellie" is a composite derived from criterion sampling with donors in interviews to collect their views and experiences. "Jamie" is also a composite of the experience of many long-term volunteers we interviewed. Amalia's work in the *aldea* is described very much as she recounted it, and was confirmed by us when we shadowed her. Additionally, there are details that come from similar programs in other locations. The stolen toilet incident happened, but the reaction of the mothers and the mayor are composites from three similar confrontations in other locations. Diane and Ellie's conversation about poverty along with Amalia's suggestions for how to create the program are an amalgam of many interviews with similar themes. The scene on the boat with Amalia and Cristobal and their search for a scholarship is what she recounted.

Amalia has verified that we kept her meaning and there was nothing misleading. In her review Diane said, "I certainly can hear the threads and themes and can relate to them, but it sounds . . . too simplistic . . . what's inside my head is way too complicated." We agree with Diane that a single story simplifies the complicated truth of her experience.

Chapter Two

The narrative in chapter two comes from scores of conversations with local staff, villagers, and foreign professionals in and around five different clinics. The description of "Lucy" and her work is based on intensity sampling over two years. Maximum variation sampling was used to encompass the multiple perspectives of the women at the river, the older and younger generations' view of hospitals and family planning, midwives, and visiting medical teams. We did multiple interviews in each of those cohorts. We were participant observers with three visiting medical teams and learned about others in interviews. We shadowed another health clinic director and interviewed staff, patients, and community members.

Other elements of fact and fiction in the narrative include the hex story, which did happen but not when a medical team was visiting. The reaction of the visitors was fictionalized, but is based on elements of our direct experience. While "Ralph" is a composite, "Brad's" words come almost entirely from his interview. "Lucy" did use the sledgehammer, oversee the "building's" reconstruction, and build relationships with the community and visiting teams.

We corroborated the accuracy of the dialogues among the women by the river by triangulating interviews, research papers, and expert review. The details about a mother and baby's death and the women's views of family planning were confirmed by a variety of indigenous mothers, several *comadronas* (midwives), and Maya spiritual guides. Additionally, the narrative is consistent with what Guatemalan educators on family planning have told us and also consistent with published research done in Guatemala by a medical anthropologist, Nicole Berry, and a U.S. midwife, Linda Walsh. (See bibliography.)

Chapter Three

All three NGO projects, staff, and program participants are portrayed as we experienced them in multiple visits and interviews. The key characters in each project have authenticated our narrative and found nothing misleading.

The story of the ten thousand dollar check was told to us in an interview and assigned to "Joe." Joe corroborated that his personality, perspective, and experience are accurate, except for the check and the story he tells about the young girl being kicked out of her house, which come from another source. Nevertheless, he says it is consistent with what he knows. While the real Joe translates and works with mission groups, his presence with the Clevelanders was how we conveyed the contrasting viewpoints from our interviews.

The people in the visiting business group from Cleveland are fictionalized but representative of our own interactions with similar groups of first-time visitors. We created their travels to and encounters with the NGOs in order to connect and contextualize interviews with scores of respondents and highlight the real strengths of the local people in this narrative.

Chapter Four

"Marta" and "Candelaria" are composites based on criterion sampling and corroborated by four women who have been loan officers in a similar situation. Likewise, the executive director and board members are composites based on interviews with many executive directors and board members. The scenes and description of micro-lending activities come from a depth of personal experience and have been authenticated by two executive directors, two founders, and additional staff, as has the story, which is fictionalized. The story of the skillet is true but happened in another women's group in another location.

Chapter Five

"Stephanie" has verified that the story in chapter five reflects the essence of her experience as a long-term volunteer; although, it has elements that come from other interviews, such as the tamales, the *pila*, and the trip to the bus stop. The cake is an example of things we've seen done to build relationships. The *curanderas* are a composite of what Stephanie told us plus our own meeting with several of them, and is consistent with information gathered in a meeting held with eight *curanderas* in their native language by our paid facilitator. "Celestina's" home is exactly like one we visited in the same village where Stephanie worked.

§

We are grateful to have been entrusted with the personal experiences that are the heart of these stories. While we recognize the limits of this book, we offer it as a starting place to which readers can add stories and insights that come from their own experiences.

BIBLIOGRAPHY

Aaker, Jerry. *Partners with the Poor: An Emerging Approach to Relief and Development*. New York: Friendship Press, 1993.

Adam, Lee Ann Joy. "Why Pay to Volunteer?" *Stanford University Transition Abroad*, July/August 2000.

Adams, Tani. "Chronic Violence and its Reproduction: Perverse Trends in Social Relations, Citizenship, and Democracy in Latin America." Woodrow Wilson International Center for Scholars, 2011. http//www.woodrowilsoncenter.org

Ak'abal, Humberto. *Raqonchi'aj, Grito* . Guatemala: Cholsamaj, 2004.

Alvarado, Elvia, and Medea Benjamin. *Don't Be Afraid, Gringo: A Honduran Woman Speaks from the Heart: The Story of Elvia Alvarado*. New York: Harper & Row, 1989.

Austin, James E., and Maria May Seitanidi. *Creating Value in Nonprofit-business Collaborations: New Thinking and Practice*. Jossey-Bass Publishers, a Wiley Brand, 2014.

Austin, James E. *The Collaboration Challenge: How Nonprofits and Businesses Succeed through Strategic Alliances*. San Francisco, CA: Jossey-Bass Publishers, 2000.

Banerjee, Abhijit V., and Esther Duflo. *Poor Economics: A Radical Rethinking of the Way to Fight Global Poverty*. New York: PublicAffairs, 2011.

Berry, Nicole S. *Unsafe Motherhood: Maternal Mortality and Subjectivity in Post-war Guatemala*. New York: Berghahn Books, 2010.

Black, Linda L., and David Stone. "Expanding the Definition of Privilege: The Concept of Social Privilege." *Journal of Multicultural Counseling and Development*, 33, no. 4 (2005): 243–55, doi:10.1002/j.2161-1912.2005. tb00020.x.

Brackley, Dean, SJ. "Meeting the Victims Falling in Love." *Salvanet, Christians for Peace in El Salvador*, January/February 2000.

Buffett, Howard G. *Forty Chances: Finding Hope in a Hungry World*. New York: Simon & Schuster, 2013.

Buffet, Peter. Op Ed: "The Charitable-Industrial Complex." *New York Times*, July 26, 2013.

Bunch, Roland. *Two Ears of Corn: A Guide to People-centered Agricultural Improvement*. Oklahoma City, OK. (5116 North Portland, Oklahoma City, 73112): World Neighbors, 1982.

Byker, Christa. "Saving The World or Patronizing It." *The Cavalier Daily* (Charlottesville, VA), March 13, 2007.

Carey, David. *Our Elders Teach Us: Maya-Kaqchikel Historical Perspectives: Xkib'ij Kan Qate' Qatata'*. Tuscaloosa: University of Alabama Press, 2001.

Carlson, Darren. "Why You Should Consider Canceling Your Short-term Mission Trips." Gospel Coalition, June 12, 2012. http:// thegospelcoalition.org/article/why-you-should-consider-cancelling-your-short-term-mission-trips

Christenson, Allen J. *Art and Society in a Highland Maya Community: The Altarpiece of Santiago Atitlán*. Austin, TX: University of Texas Press, 2001.

Clinton, Bill. *Giving: How Each of Us Can Change the World*. New York: Knopf, 2007.

Coles, Robert. *The Call of Service: A Witness to Idealism*. Boston: Houghton Mifflin, 1993.

Collier, Paul. *The Bottom Billion: Why the Poorest Countries Are failing and What Can Be Done About It*. Oxford: Oxford University Press, 2007.

Collins, Joseph, Stefano DeZerega, and Zahara Heckscher. *How to Live Your Dream of Volunteering Overseas*. New York: Penguin Books, 2002.

Corbett, Steve, and Brian Fikkert. *When Helping Hurts: How to Alleviate Poverty without Hurting the Poor—and Yourself*. Chicago, IL: Moody Publishers, 2009.

Coster, Helen. "Can Venture Capital Save the World?" *Forbes Magazine*, December 19, 2011.

Crisp, Nigel. *Turning the World Upside Down: The Search for Global Health in the Twenty-first Century*. London: Royal Society of Medicine Press, 2010.

Crump, J. A., and J. Sugarman. "Ethical Considerations for Short-term Experiences by Trainees in Global Health." *JAMA: The Journal of the American Medical Association*, 300, no. 12 (2008): 1456–458, doi:10.1001/jama.300.12.1456.

Daley-Harris, Sam. *Pathways Out of Poverty: Innovations in Microfinance for the Poorest Families*. Bloomfield, CT: Kumarian Press, 2002.

Desimone, Elizabeth. *Guatemala in My Blood: How Nursing in Remote Jungle Villages Revolutionized My Life*. Seattle, WA: Travels in Guatemala Press, 2009.

Diggs, David. "We See From Where We Stand." Faith & Money Network. http://www.faithandmoneynetwork.org/sites/g/files/g759651/f/201403/We%20See%20Things%20From%20Where%20We%20Stand-David%20Diggs.pdf.

Donnelly, John. *A Twist of Faith: An American Christian's Quest to Help Orphans in Africa*. Boston: Beacon Press, 2012.

Easterly, Professor William. *The Tyranny of Experts*. Washington: Basic Civitas Books, 2013.

Easterly, William. *The White Man's Burden: Why the West's Efforts to Aid the Rest Have Done So Much Ill and So Little Good*. New York: Penguin Press, 2006.

Elmer, Duane. *Cross-Cultural Connections: Stepping Out and Fitting In Around the World*. Downers Grove, IL: InterVarsity Press, 2002.

Engen, Van, and Jo Ann. "The Cost of Short-term Missions." *The Other Side*, January 1, 2000.

Escobar, Arturo. *Encountering Development: The Making and Unmaking of the Third World*. Princeton, NJ: Princeton University Press, 1995.

Farmer, Paul, and Haun Saussy. *Partner to the Poor: A Paul Farmer Reader*. Berkeley: University of California Press, 2010.

Farmer, Paul, and Jonathan Weigel. *To Repair the World: Paul Farmer Speaks to the World*. Berkley, CA, London: University of California Press, 2013.

Farmer, Paul. *Pathologies of Power: Health, Human Rights, and the New War on the Poor*. Berkeley: University of California Press, 2003.

Fitzpatrick, Laura. "Vacationing Like Brangelina: Does Volunteer Tourism Do Any Good?" *Time Magazine*, July 26, 2007.

Freire, Paulo, and Myra Bergman. Ramos. *Pedagogy of the Oppressed*. London: Penguin, 1972.

Gawande, Atul. "Slow Ideas: Some Innovations Spread Fast. How Do You Speed the Ones That Don't?" *The New Yorker*, July 29, 2013.

Geitz, Elizabeth Rankin. *I Am That Child: Changing Hearts and Changing the World*. Harrisburg, PA: Morehouse Pub., 2012.

Gibb, Jack R. "Is Help Helpful?" *Forum, Journal of the Association of Professional Directors of YMCAs in the U.S.*, February 1964.

Gladwell, Malcolm. "The Gift of Doubt, Albert O. Hirschman and the Power of Failure." *The New Yorker*, June 24, 2013.

Gourevitch, Philip. "The Monkey and the Fish: Can Greg Carr Save an African Ecosystem." *The New Yorker*, December 21 and 28, 2009.

Green, Tyler, Heidi Green, Jean Scandlyn, and Andrew Kestler. "Perceptions of Short-term Medical Volunteer Work: A Qualitative

Study in Guatemala." *Globalization and Health*, 5, no. 1 (2009): 4, doi:10.1186/1744-8603-5-4.

Hall, Edward T. *Beyond Culture*. Garden City, NY: Anchor Press, 1976.

Hessler, Peter. "Village Voice: The Peace Corps's Brightest Hope." *The New Yorker*, December 20 and 27, 2010.

Hilfiker, David. "The Limits of Charity." *The Other Side*, September 1, 2000.

Hofstede, Gert Jan., Paul Pedersen, and Geert H. Hofstede. *Exploring Culture: Exercises, Stories, and Synthetic Cultures*. Yarmouth, Me.: Intercultural Press, 2002.

Hogan, Tori. *Beyond Good Intentions: A Journey into the Realities of International Aid*. Berkeley, CA: Seal Press, 2012.

Huebsch, Dave. *Village Assignment: True Stories of Humor, Adventure and Drama in Guatemala's Highland Villages*. Little Falls, MN: Highlight Pub., 2004.

Human Rights Office of the Archdiocese of Guatemala. *Guatemala: Never Again!* Maryknoll, NY: Orbis Books, 1999. This is the abbreviated English version of *Guatemala, Nunca Más*.

Illich, Ivan. "To Hell With Good Intentions." Speech, Cuernavaca, Mexico: Conference on InterAmerican Student Projects (CIASP), April 20, 1968.

Jesus, John E. "Ethical Challenges and Considerations of Short-term International Medical Initiatives: An Excursion to Ghana as a Case Study." *Annals of Emergency Medicine*, 55, no. 1 (2010): 17–22, doi:10.1016/j.annemergmed.2009.07.014.

Kagawa-Singer, Marjorie, and Shaheen Kassim-Lakha. "A Strategy to Reduce Cross-cultural Miscommunication and Increase the Likelihood of Improving Health Outcomes." *Academic Medicine*, 78, no. 6 (2003): 577–87, doi:10.1097/00001888-200306000-00006.

Karlan, Dean S., and Jacob Appel. *More than Good Intentions: How a New Economics Is Helping to Solve Global Poverty*. New York: Dutton, 2011.

Keizer, Garret. *Help: The Original Human Dilemma*. San Francisco: Harper San Francisco, 2004.

Kenny, Charles. *Getting Better: Why Global Development is Succeeding*. New York: Basic Books, 2011.

Kidder, Tracy. *Mountains beyond Mountains*. New York: Random House, 2003.

Kolker, Claudia. *The Immigrant Advantage: What We Can Learn from Newcomers to America about Health, Happiness and Hope*. New York: Free Press, 2011.

Koll, Karla Ann. "Taking Wolves among Lambs: Some Thoughts on Training for Short-term Mission Facilitation." *International Bulletin of Missionary Research*, April 1, 2010.

Koss-Feder, Laura. "Giving Back: An Investment with Meaning." *Time Magazine*, March 29, 2007.

Krasnoff, Margo J., ed. *Building Partnerships in the Americas: A Guide for Global Health Workers*. Hanover, N.H.: Dartmouth University Press, 2013.

Krishna, Anirudh. *One Illness Away: Why People Become Poor and How They Escape Poverty*. Oxford: Oxford University Press, 2010.

Kristof, Nicholas D., and Sheryl WuDunn. *Half the Sky: Turning Oppression into Opportunity for Women Worldwide*. New York: Alfred A. Knopf, 2009.

Lane, Patty. *A Beginner's Guide to Crossing Cultures: Making Friends in a Multicultural World*. Downers Grove, IL: InterVarsity Press, 2002.

Lanier, Sarah A. *Foreign to Familiar: A Guide to Understanding Hot- and Cold-climate Cultures*. Hagerstown, MD: McDougal Pub., 2000.

Lederleitner, Mary. *Cross-Cultural Partners: Navigating the Complexities of Money and Mission*. Intervarsity Press, 2010.

Leonard, Gavin. "Rethinking Volunteerism in America." World Volunteer Web, February 2006. http://www.worldvolunteerweb.org/news-views/viewpoints/doc/rethinking-volunteerism-in-america.html

Little, Christopher. "When Two Bikes Split a Church: The Powerful Effect of an Act of Generosity." *Mission Frontiers Crossing Boundaries,* November 1, 2000.

Little, Walter, and Timothy Smith. *Mayas in Post-war Guatemala Harvest of Violence, Revisited.* Tuscaloosa: University of Alabama Press, 2009.

Livermore, David A. *Cultural Intelligence: Improving Your CQ to Engage Our Multicultural World.* Grand Rapids, MI: Baker Academic, 2009.

Livermore, David A. *Serving with Eyes Wide Open: Doing Short-term Missions with Cultural Intelligence.* Grand Rapids, MI: Baker Books, 2006.

Lupton, Robert D. *Compassion, Justice and the Christian Life: Rethinking Ministry to the Poor.* Ventura, CA: Regal Books, 2007.

Lough, Benjamin J. *International Volunteering from the United States between 2004 and 2012.* Washington University in St. Louis. Research brief, 2013. CSD publication #13–14.

Lupton, Robert D. *Toxic Charity: How Churches and Charities Hurt Those They Help (and How to Reverse It).* New York, NY: Harper One, 2011.

MacDonald, Neil. *Cautionary Tales for Development Folk.* Text copyright 2013 Neil MacDonald

Mackintosh, Peggy. "White Privilege: Unpacking the Invisible Knapsack." *Peace and Freedom,* 1989.

Maupin, Jonathan Nathaniel. "'Fruit of the Accords': Healthcare Reform and Civil Participation in Highland Guatemala." *Social Science & Medicine,* 68, no. 8 (2009): 1456–463, doi:10.1016/j.socscimed.2009.01.045.

McKee, Jonathan R., and Thomas W. McKee. *The New Breed: Understanding & Equipping the 21st-century Volunteer.* Loveland, CO: Group, 2008.

McMillon, Bill, Doug Cutchins, and Anne Geissinger. *Volunteer Vacations: Short-term Adventures That Will Benefit You and Others.* Chicago, IL: Chicago Review Press, 2009.

Melander, Veronica. *The Hour of God?: People in Guatemala Confronting Political Evangelicalism and Counterinsurgency (1976–1990).* Uppsala: Swedish Institute of Missionary Research, 1999.

"'Memory of Silence' U.N. Historical Clarification Commission Issues Report on Human Rights Abuses in Guatemala; U.S. Policies Implicated." *Foreign Policy Bulletin*, 10, no. 02 (1999): 67. doi:10.1017/S1052703600002239.

Molesky-Poz, Jean. *Contemporary Maya Spirituality: The Ancient Ways Are Not Lost*. Austin: University of Texas Press, 2006.

Moller, Jonathan, and Ricardo Falla. *Our Culture is Our Resistance: Repression, Refuge and Healing in Guatemala*. New York: Power House Books, 2004.

Moyo, Dambisa. *Dead Aid: Why Aid is Not Working and How There is a Better Way for Africa*. New York: Farrar, Straus and Giroux, 2009.

Myers, Bryant L. *Walking with the Poor: Principles and Practices of Transformational Development*. Maryknoll, NY: Orbis Books, 1999.

Nocera, Joe. "Fighting Poverty, and Critics." Editorial. *The New York Times*, September 2, 2013.

Novogratz, Jacqueline. *The Blue Sweater: Bridging the Gap between Rich and Poor in an Interconnected World*. New York: Rodale, 2009.

Nussbaum, Stan. *American Cultural Baggage: How to Recognize and Deal with It*. Maryknoll, NY: Orbis Books, 2005.

Nussbaum, Stan. *A Reader's Guide to Transforming Mission*. Maryknoll, NY: Orbis Books, 2005.

Parker, Ian. "The Poverty Lab: Transforming Developmental Economics One Experiment at a Time." *The New Yorker*, May 17, 2010.

Perkins, John. *Beyond Charity: The Call to Christian Community Development*. Grand Rapids, MI: Baker Books, 1993.

Philbrook, Burnham. "A Philosophy of Service." Global Volunteers, 2006.

Polak, Paul. *Out of Poverty: What Works When Traditional Approaches Fail*. San Francisco, CA: Berrett-Koehler, 2008.

Prakash, Madhu Suri, and Gustavo Esteva. *Escaping Education: Living as Learning within Grassroots Cultures*. New York: P. Lang, 1998.

Presler, Titus Leonard. *Going Global with God: Reconciling Mission in a World of Difference*. New York: Morehouse Pub., 2010.

Priest, Robert J. *Effective Engagement in Short-term Missions: Doing It Right!* Pasadena, CA: William Carey Library, 2008.

Priest, Robert J., Terry Dischinger, Steve Rasmussen, C. M. Brownet. "Researching the Short-term Mission Movement." Research paper (2006): p. 444, www.academia.edu

Purcell-Gates, Victoria, and Robin Waterman. *Now We Read, We See, We Speak: Portrait of Literacy Development in an Adult Freirean-based Class*. Mahwah, NJ: L. Erlbaum Associates, Publishers, 2000.

Rah, Soong-Chan. *Many Colors: Cultural Intelligence for a Changing Church*. Chicago: Moody Publishers, 2010.

Rahnema, Majid, and Victoria Bawtree. *The Post-development Reader*. London: Zed Books, 1997.

Roberts, M. "Duffle Bag Medicine." *JAMA: The Journal of the American Medical Association*, 295, no. 13 (2006): 1491–492, doi:10.1001/jama.295.13.1491.

Sachs, Wolfgang. *The Development Dictionary: A Guide to Knowledge as Power*. London: Zed Books, 1992.

Salmen, Lawrence F., and Eileen Kane. *Bridging Diversity: Participatory Learning for Responsive Development*. Washington, DC: World Bank, 2006.

Salmen, Lawrence F. *Listen to the People: Participant-observer Evaluation of Development Projects*. New York: Published for the World Bank by Oxford University Press, 1987.

Sanford, Victoria. *Buried Secrets: Truth and Human Rights in Guatemala*. New York: Palgrave Macmillan, 2003.

Schulz, Kathryn. *Being Wrong: Adventures in the Margin of Error*. New York: Ecco, 2010.

Schwartz, Glenn. *When Charity Destroys Dignity: Overcoming Unhealthy Dependency in the Christian Movement: A Compendium*. Lancaster, PA: World Mission Associates, 2007.

Sen, Amartya. *Development as Freedom*. New York: Knopf, 1999.

Shapiro, Ruth A. *The Real Problem Solvers: Social Entrepreneurs in America*. Stanford Business Books, 2012.

Sichel, Benjamin. "I've Come to Help: Can Tourism and Altruism Mix?" *Briarpatch Magazine*, November 2006.

Smissen, John. "Post-war Guatemala Faces Many Challenges." *Presbyterian Outlook*, vol. 184, no. 33, October 7, 2002.

Smith, Dennis. "Do No Harm." Sarasota, FL: Peace River Presbytery, November 16, 2006.

Smith, Dennis. "A Latin American Pilgrimage: Reflections on Media, Religion and Culture." Dean Rusk Lecture, Davidson College (Davidson, NC), November 16, 2009.

Stengel, Richard. "Doing Well by Doing Good." *Time Magazine*, September 10, 2009.

Stengel, Richard. "A Time to Serve." *Time Magazine*, September 10, 2007.

Stone, Suzanne. *Volunteering around the Globe: Life-changing Travel Adventures*. Herndon, VA: Capital Books, 2008.

Storti, Craig. *The Art of Crossing Cultures*. Yarmouth, ME: Intercultural Press, 1990.

Storti, Craig. *Figuring Foreigners Out: A Practical Guide*. Yarmouth, Me.: Intercultural Press, 1999.

Tannen, D. "The Pragmatics of Cross-Cultural Communication." *Applied Linguistics*, 5, no. 3 (1984): 189–95, doi:10.1093/applin/5.3.189.

Thomas, Zach. *Weaving Common Hope: A Future for Guatemalan Children*. Bloomington, ID: 1st Books Library, 2003.

Till, Brian. "God's Surgeons in Africa." *The Atlantic*, December 2012. theatlantic.com/health/archive/2012/12/gods-surgeons-in-africa/26635

Twersky, Fay, Phil Buchanan, and Valerie Threlsall. "Listening to Those Who Matter Most, The Beneficiaries." *Stanford Social Innovation Review*, Spring 2013.

Ujpán, Ignacio Bizarro, and James D. Sexton. *Ignacio: The Diary of a Maya Indian of Guatemala*. Philadelphia: University of Pennsylvania Press, 1992.

Ver Beek, Kurt Alan. "The Impact of Short-term Missions: A Case Study of House Construction in Honduras After Hurricane Mitch," *Missiology*, 34, no. 4 (October, 2006): p. 477–495.

"Volunteers Go Into Action With the Means and the Will to Give Back," *Time Magazine*, April 16, 2007.

Wilkinson, Daniel. *Silence on the Mountain: Stories of Terror, Betrayal, and Forgetting in Guatemala*. Boston: Houghton Mifflin, 2002.

Yemma, John. "The Samaritan's Dilemma: How Best to Help?" *The Christian Science Monitor* (Boston), January 10, 2011.

ACKNOWLEDGMENTS

We are indebted to all the Guatemalans and foreigners who shared their experiences with us. They enriched our lives and broadened our perspectives. There would be no book without them. They are street kids and Maya spiritual guides; backpackers and anthropologists; midwives and doctors; philanthropists and missionaries; board members and executive directors; NGO staff and their clients; birdwatchers and coffee growers; teachers and preachers; farmers and weavers; students and expats; market vendors and volcanologists; human rights workers and cooks; gardeners and internet techs; tourists and *tuk-tuk* drivers; and volunteers of every size, shape, and age. We thank you, one and all.

When we started writing about how all those different lives intersect in Guatemala, we wanted to make all their voices sing. It was clear we needed help. We thank each one who has provided their expertise and been both patient and persistent with us. First, Kathleen Hirsch and Ken Achity's critiques of our initial draft got us rolling. For four years Kristin Patterson put her writer-coach skills and deft red pencil to work, pushing us to rewrite one more time with graceful comments, questions, and suggestions. She gets our prize for patience and perspicacity. More recently, Meg Lemke brought her well-honed professional editing skills to help us get the manuscript ready for publication. We appreciate her extraordinary insights, balanced viewpoint, and support as we sought to do something outside the box.

Among those who helped us with our interviews, we want to recognize Eli Morris, who did both typing and translation from Spanish to English. José Aguilar and Fredy Upan did interviews in Tz'utujil and Kaqchikel and translated them into Spanish. Norma Bajan and Maria Ixbalán interviewed in Kaqchikel and translated into Spanish; they also trusted us with their own stories, collected others from their neighbors, and gave feedback when we endeavored to give tone and feeling to Maya realities. Liz Green typed English translations across the airwaves by phone and Skype with good will and amazing speed. Betty Case proofread the entire book with enthusiasm, an incredible eye for detail, and amazing speed.

This book sprouted in part due to generous seed money from our friends Helen Harper, Mary Ann Kuntz, and Bev Lawrence.

Off-season loans of wonderful homes in the U.S. gave us inspired venues for intense work that we called "lockdown." Our abundant thanks to Carol Bloomberg, Brad Googins, Karen and Phil Larson, Meg and Michael Leonard, the Loretto Community, Charlie and Eleanor Skipsey, Priscilla Smith, and Penny and Phil Weinstein. We are also abundantly grateful to Marianne Lee and Wyllis Terry, Judy Sadlier and Gene Bundige for their hospitality in Guatemala.

There are more people than we can name who have given us feedback, which has helped us understand how our words fall on different ears. But chief among them are: Larry Dressler, Leeann Heinbaugh, Diane Nicholls, Peter Rohloff, Bill Scott, Priscilla Smith, and Penny and Phil Weinstein. They read every chapter and commented on multiple drafts over six years. We are eternally grateful for their insights.

We also appreciate comments, critiques, and suggestions at various stages from: Daniela Abadi, Norma Bajan, Nancy Bingham, Margaret Blood, Betty Case, Marleny Castillo Rodus, Joanne Coakley, Julio Cochoy, John Costello, Rebecca Cutter, Gael Dhanens, Alcira Forero Pena, Shari Friedman, Jessica Gonzales, Ted Gaiser, Bob Graham, John Haskins, Katharine Hobart, Robert Hinshaw, Maralise Hood, Pär Ivarsson, Ruth Kasle, Liz and Stephen Kendrick, Sarah Kennedy, Karla Koll, Mary Ann Kuntz, Barbara Lee, Helena Mariposa, Molly Marsh, Ann McClenahan, Hilda Mendoza, Marcus Naugle, Bonnie O'Neil, Erica Pang, Julio Quan, Judith and Warren Radtke, Bev Reed, Kendra Rickerby, Caitlin Scott, Mary Lyons Scott,q Linda Smith, Stephanie Spellers, Sally Susnowitz, Pat Torpie, Andre and Lyle Waldman, Jen Wenz, Laura Wheelock, Eden Williams, Sandy

Younghans, and Bob Zuber.

There are other people who have supported us in Guatemala. They are dear to us for a myriad of reasons: Rick and Betty Adams, Richard and Sylvia Hutchinson, Jaime Zaccagnini, Marco Reuters, Ana Vivar, Eloin and Gael Dhanens, Salvador Raxtun, Victor Mariano Joj Sahón, and Josefina Lopez Cumes.

Finally, we're grateful to family near and far for unwavering support and endless solicitousness as to how the book was coming, long after they'd given up reading endless drafts: Amalia Stouse Bell, Christopher J. Bell, Elizabeth Scully Krizek, Alex Krizek, Lukas Krizek, Aline Koppel, Brian Scully, and Dennis Scully.

ABOUT THE AUTHORS

Connie Newton has been living and working in Central America, off and on for over fifty years, currently residing half the year in Guatemala. She worked as a human rights activist, accompanier, and educator during the decades of violence in Central America. For ten years she organized and facilitated cross-cultural immersion-learning trips in the U.S. and Latin America. She founded an experiential education program for a microcredit organization in Guatemala, whose board she served on for ten years. In that role she developed trusting relationships with indigenous women in mountain villages, who have provided important insights and connections for doing good in another culture.

Fran Early has been an organizer for the Greater Boston Interfaith Organization since 1996, experiencing the political power that comes from building relationships across the many cultural and religious lines that divide metro Boston. Always a change agent, Fran retired from The Prudential after thirty years in human resources, public affairs, and operations management. She led a Total Quality Process, which recognized employee's wisdom at all levels, resulting in improved service and reduced costs. Long drawn to indigenous cultures, she has lived a couple of months each year in Guatemala for the past decade, and she has done home stays with indigenous families in both rural and urban settings.